Teens Emotional Regulation

A step-by-step method to identify triggers, decode emotions, build confident responses, and take back your inner power

Agnes Blake

Hw Premier Publishing LLC

Library of Congress Control Number: 9798993423241

Contents

Introduction

Georgia's hands clamp the steering wheel, knuckles pale. Her heart slams against her ribs. Just twenty minutes ago, she was laughing with friends, excited for the weekend. Then she opened the group chat.

She'd shared her honest take on the drama between two friends—she was thoughtful, calm, and well-intentioned. She hit send and waited.

Silence.

No reactions. No replies. Just those brutal little read receipts proving everyone had seen it.

Now her thoughts spiral: *Did I say something wrong? Did I overstep? Are they talking about me somewhere else?* Her chest tightens, her breathing shrinks, and tears gather in the school parking lot over a single message.

A voice in her head whispers that something must be wrong with her for caring this much.

If any of that feels familiar, you're in the right place.

That racing heart, the overthinking, the fear of being "too much"—none of it is a flaw. None of it is weakness. And you're absolutely not alone.

You're Not Broken

This book isn't here to "fix" you or turn you into someone quieter, calmer, or more "normal." You're not broken. You feel deeply, and that's part of your wiring.

Its purpose is to validate what you're experiencing and give you tools to work with your emotions instead of battling them. Every feeling—anxiety, anger, sadness, excitement—is information your mind uses to navigate a complicated world.

The goal isn't to feel less. It's to trust yourself more.

Your emotional intensity can become a strength you rely on. This journey is about empowerment and building skills you can use in everyday life—whether you're dealing with panic in a school bathroom, friend drama, or conflict at home.

Who This Book Is For

Feel "too much,"

You cry at movies, get excited easily, or feel crushed when plans suddenly change. People call you "dramatic" or "sensitive," and you're tired of apologizing for it.

Battle social anxiety

Lunch alone feels safer. Parties feel like pressure. You replay conversations at night and worry about every word you said.

Feel overwhelmed by daily pressures

School, friendships, family expectations, and constant comparison pile until everything feels like too much. "Just relax" doesn't help.

Want real confidence

You want to show up as your true self without constantly wondering whether you're too much .

Feel misunderstood by adults

They care, but they don't always understand what you're going through. Seeking help shows courage and insight.

Why This Book Is Different

Many teen self-help books feel out of touch. This one doesn't.

• Real teen scenarios—things you actually deal with.• Private exercises—no sharing required.• Simple brain science—clear and easy to understand.• Real-time tools—techniques you can use immediately.• No toxic positivity—no pretending things are fine when they aren't.• Strength-based approach—your sensitivity is a superpower.

What You'll Learn

Think of this book as emotional strength training—steady, practical, and designed to help you grow.

You'll learn how to:

• Understand why your emotions feel so intense• Identify what you're truly feeling• Quiet your inner critic• Handle comparison and social media pressure• Manage school stress and academic anxiety• Communicate clearly during conflicts• Show up authentically even with social anxiety• Bounce back from rejection and disappointment• Build a stronger sense of who you are

Each chapter builds on the last, but you can jump to whatever you need most.Panicking? Go to grounding techniques.Friend drama? Head to conflict skills.

Use the book in whatever way supports you best.

Before You Begin

Grab a notebook, journal, or the notes app on your phone—something private and just for you. Write, record voice notes, or think through the prompts silently—whatever works.

The only requirement is honesty with yourself

Chapter 1: Emotion Basics

Why You're Not "Too Much"

Your emotions aren't broken—your brain is literally under construction. The teenage brain is going through massive renovations, with the emotional center (amygdala) fully developed while the rational control center (prefrontal cortex) won't finish construction until around age 25. This means you're experiencing adult-level emotions with a brain that's still learning how to regulate them effectively.

Think of it like living in a house during a major remodel. The electricity might work perfectly in the kitchen, but the wiring in the living room is still being installed. Your emotional responses are firing at full capacity, but the systems that help you process and manage those feelings are still being built.

Here's what's actually happening in your brain:

- Your emotional brain develops faster than your logical brain, creating an intensity gap that's completely normal
- Hormonal fluctuations during adolescence amplify emotional responses, making feelings hit harder and faster
- Research shows 70% of teens report feeling overwhelmed by their emotions at least once a week—you're in the majority, not the minority

Isabel used to think she was "broken" because she would cry during movies that barely made her friends blink. She felt embarrassed when she got teary-eyed during a school assembly about kindness, while everyone else seemed unaffected. Learning that her brain was naturally wired to feel more intensely helped her realize that her emotional depth wasn't a flaw—it was evidence of a developing mind that would eventually become her superpower for connecting with others.

Emotional intensity isn't a weakness. It's information.

When you feel overwhelmed by anger after a small criticism, that's your brain's alarm system working overtime. When you experience crushing disappointment over a canceled plan, that's your developing neural pathways learning to process loss. When you feel anxious about social situations, that's your mind trying to protect you from potential rejection.

Your emotions serve specific purposes, even when they feel chaotic:

- Anger signals that something important to you has been threatened or violated
- Sadness helps you process loss and signals to others that you need support
- Anxiety alerts you to potential challenges and motivates you to prepare
- Joy reinforces positive experiences and strengthens social bonds
- Fear protects you from real or perceived dangers

The problem isn't that you have these emotions. The problem is that no one taught you how to work with them.

Ethan struggled with explosive anger that seemed to come out of nowhere. His parents would tell him to "calm down" or "control yourself," but he did not know how to actually do that. Once he learned that anger was his brain's way of signaling that his boundaries had been crossed, he could start paying attention to the earlier warning signs—the tight chest, the racing thoughts, the urge to clench his fists. This awareness gave him a chance to respond instead of just react.

Most teens receive the message that powerful emotions are problems to be fixed rather than information to be understood. Society tells you to "get over it" or "toughen up" without teaching you the actual skills to process what you're feeling. This creates shame around normal human experiences.

Your emotional system is actually incredibly sophisticated. It processes millions of pieces of information every second, scanning for threats, opportunities, and social cues. That it sometimes gets overwhelmed doesn't mean it's defective—it means it's working exactly as designed for a brain that's still developing.

Understanding this biological reality changes everything. Instead of fighting against your emotions or judging yourself for having them, you can learn to work with your natural wiring. This doesn't mean letting emotions control your actions, but developing the skills to recognize, understand, and respond to them effectively.

Pinpointing Your Emotions with the Mood Wheel

Moving beyond "I feel bad" or "I'm fine" gives you power over your emotional experience. When you can specifically name what you're feeling, you activate the thinking part of your brain, which naturally calms the emotional storm. This process, called "affect labeling," literally reduces the intensity of overwhelming feelings by engaging your prefrontal cortex—the same brain region we discussed earlier that's still under construction.

Think of emotions like colors. Saying "I feel bad" is like pointing at a sunset and saying, "It's colored." You're missing the rich oranges, deep purples, soft pinks, and golden yellows that make up the complete picture. Your emotions are similar in complexity and nuance.

The mood wheel is a practical tool that breaks down the broad categories of emotions into specific, actionable descriptions.

Instead of swimming in a sea of "upset," you can pinpoint whether you're feeling:

- Specific emotion words help your brain process feelings more effectively than vague descriptions
- A visual mood wheel with emoji representations makes it easier to quickly identify complex emotions
- Practice with the wheel builds emotional vocabulary, giving you more precise tools for self-awareness and communication with others

Derek discovered that what he always called "anger" was actually a mix of disappointment, frustration, and hurt. When his friend canceled plans last minute, instead of just saying, "I'm mad," he used the mood wheel and realized he felt "let down" and "unimportant." This clarity helped him have an actual conversation with his friend instead of just staying silent and resentful.

Here's how the mood wheel works in practice:

The Core Emotions (Center of the Wheel):

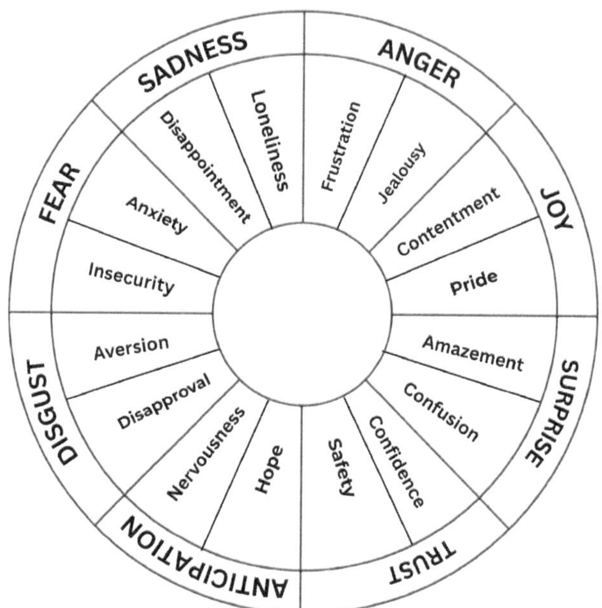

Here is what the Emotional Mood Wheel looks like. Use it as a visual reference as you read through this section.

- Happy
- Sad
- Angry
- Afraid
- Surprised
- Disgusted

The Specific Variations (Outer Ring):

From "sad" you might identify disappointed, lonely, hopeless, grief-stricken, melancholy, or dejected.

From "angry" you could be frustrated, irritated, furious, resentful, annoyed, or outraged.

From "afraid" you might feel anxious, worried, terrified, nervous, panicked, or uneasy.

Mia used to tell her parents she was "fine" even when she was clearly struggling. After learning about the mood wheel, she realized that "fine" was often code for "overwhelmed and confused." She started checking in with herself using the wheel and discovered she could identify specific feelings like "stressed about expectations," "lonely in social situations," or "excited but nervous about changes."

The wheel becomes especially powerful when you're experiencing multiple emotions at once, which happens more often than you might think. You might feel excited about a new opportunity while also feeling anxious about the unknown. You could be happy about a friend's success while simultaneously feeling envious. These complex emotional combinations are completely normal.

Using the Mood Wheel Step-by-Step:

1. Stop and breathe when you notice you're having a strong emotional reaction

2. Ask yourself: "What's the core emotion I'm feeling right now?"

3. Look at the wheel and identify the broad category first

4. Narrow it down to the specific variation that fits best

5. Check for additional emotions that might be present at the same time

Research shows that people who can accurately identify their emotions have better relationships, make clearer decisions, and experience fewer overwhelming emotional episodes. When you can say, "I'm feeling excluded and embarrassed" instead of "I feel terrible," you give yourself and others specific information to work with.

This precision becomes the foundation for everything else you'll learn in this book. In the next chapter, we'll explore how self-doubt and sensitivity often mask themselves as other emotions, making the mood wheel an essential tool for uncovering what's really happening beneath the surface.

The goal isn't to eliminate difficult emotions—it's to understand them clearly enough that you can respond thoughtfully rather than just react impulsively. When you know exactly what you're feeling, you can understand why you're feeling it and what you might need to address the underlying cause.

Practice with the mood wheel regularly, especially during calm moments, so it becomes second nature when emotions run high.

Mapping Your Emotional Landmines

Your triggers are like emotional landmines—specific situations, words, or experiences that instantly flood you with intense feelings. Understanding your personal trigger map helps you prepare for challenging moments and respond intentionally instead of just reacting. Everyone's triggers are different based on their unique experiences and sensitivities, which means your emotional landscape is completely personal to you.

Think of triggers as your brain's alarm system going off when it detects something that previously caused you pain or stress. Your amygdala, that emotional center we discussed earlier, doesn't distinguish between actual threats and perceived ones. It just remembers "this situation equals danger" and floods your system with fight-or-flight chemicals before your rational brain can even process what's happening.

Understanding the Three Main Categories of Triggers:

- Environmental triggers include specific locations, sounds, or times of day that affect your emotional state
- Social triggers involve certain people, conversation topics, or group dynamics that consistently upset you
- Digital triggers encompass specific apps, notification sounds, or online situations that spike your anxiety or anger

Diana realized that her biggest trigger was being interrupted mid-sentence. It made her feel invisible and unimportant, often leading either to shutting down completely or snapping at whoever cut her off. Once she identified this pattern, she started using phrases like "I wasn't finished" or "Let me complete my thought" to advocate for herself calmly instead of either exploding or disappearing.

Environmental Triggers:

Your physical surroundings can dramatically affect your emotional state. Crowded hallways might make you feel claustrophobic and anxious. Certain smells could instantly transport you back to an embarrassing memory. The sound of your phone buzzing during the late hours might trigger panic about what bad news might be waiting.

Frank discovered that the fluorescent lighting in his school's cafeteria consistently made him feel agitated and overwhelmed. He couldn't explain why the lunch period always felt so stressful until he connected the harsh lighting to his sensory sensitivity. Now he sits near the windows when possible or wears sunglasses briefly to adjust his eyes before eating.

Social Triggers:

These involve interactions with people that consistently spark intense emotions. Being excluded from conversations, hearing certain phrases like "you're too sensitive," or dealing with specific personality types can all serve as social landmines. Family dynamics often contain the most powerful social triggers because these relationships carry the deepest emotional history.

Common social triggers include:

- Feeling judged or criticized
- Being compared to siblings or friends
- Experiencing dismissive responses to your feelings
- Dealing with passive-aggressive behavior

- Facing pressure to perform or be perfect

Digital Triggers:

In our connected world, technology creates entirely new categories of emotional landmines. The ping of notifications during family time might trigger anxiety about missing out. Seeing certain people's posts could instantly flood you with comparison and inadequacy. Even specific apps or websites can become associated with negative emotional experiences.

Mapping Your Personal Triggers:

Start paying attention to moments when your emotional response seems bigger than the situation warrants. Misunderstanding often signal that a trigger has been activated. Keep track of:

- What exactly happened right before the intense emotion?
- Where were you, and who was around?
- What physical sensations did you notice first?
- What thoughts immediately ran through your mind?

Diana kept a trigger journal for two weeks and discovered that her anxiety always spiked when she heard her parents talking quietly behind closed doors. This pattern traced back to a time when hushed conversations meant bad news was coming. Understanding this connection helped her realize that current quiet conversations weren't threats requiring immediate panic.

The Power of Recognition:

You can't control when triggers appear, but you can control your response once you recognize what's happening. When you identify your emotional landmines, you gain the ability to pause and ask yourself: "Is this situation actually dangerous, or is my brain remembering something from the past?"

This awareness becomes the foundation for the emotional regulation skills we'll build throughout this book. In Chapter 2, we'll explore how self-doubt and sensitivity often amplify trigger responses, creating an internal battle that can feel overwhelming. Understanding your triggers now prepares you to navigate that inner conflict with greater clarity and confidence.

The goal isn't to eliminate triggers completely—that's impossible and unnecessary. Instead, you're building the self-awareness to respond thoughtfully when they activate, rather than being hijacked by automatic reactions.

When Blue Feelings Turn Deeper

Everyone has rough days, but persistent sadness that interferes with daily life for over two weeks might signal something that needs professional support. Learning to distinguish between temporary emotional dips and potential mental health concerns isn't about self-diagnosis—it's about knowing when to seek additional help beyond self-care strategies.

Understanding this difference is crucial because it helps you respond appropriately to what you're experiencing. Just as you wouldn't ignore a broken bone, persistent emotional pain deserves attention and care. Your developing brain, which we've discussed throughout this chapter, can sometimes struggle with chemical imbalances that affect mood regulation beyond normal teenage emotional intensity.

Recognizing the Warning Signs:

- Temporary sadness usually has an identifiable cause and improves within a few days with rest and self-care
- Persistent depression often includes changes in sleep, appetite, energy levels, and interest in activities you usually enjoy
- Physical symptoms like constant fatigue, headaches, or stomach issues can accompany mental health struggles and shouldn't be ignored

Marcus went through a month where everything felt harder than usual. Getting out of bed was exhausting; he stopped texting his friends back, and even his favorite video games felt pointless. Initially, he thought he was just stressed about midterms, but when the feelings persisted even after the tests ended, he recognized this might be more than typical stress. Talking to the school counselor helped him understand that what he was experiencing was common and treatable, not a personal weakness.

Normal Sadness vs. Concerning Patterns:

Normal sadness tends to:

- Have a clear trigger or cause

- Come and go in waves
- Allow you to still enjoy some activities
- Improve with time, sleep, and social connection
- Feel manageable most of the time

Concerning patterns include:

- Feeling hopeless about the future
- Losing interest in everything you usually enjoy
- Significant changes in eating or sleeping patterns
- Thoughts of self-harm or suicide
- Feeling emotionally numb or empty
- Difficulty concentrating that affects school performance

The mood wheel we learned about earlier becomes especially important here. If you're consistently identifying emotions in the "sad" category like hopeless, worthless, or empty for extended periods, that's valuable information to share with a trusted adult.

Physical Signs Matter Too:

Mental health struggles often show up in your body before you recognize them emotionally. Your brain and body are connected through complex systems, so emotional pain frequently manifests as physical symptoms.

- Constant exhaustion even with adequate sleep

- Frequent headaches or muscle tension
- Stomach problems or changes in appetite
- Getting sick more often than usual
- Feeling physically heavy or sluggish

Ava noticed she had been getting headaches every day for three weeks. She assumed it was stress from school, but when she tracked her mood using the wheel, she realized she'd been feeling "defeated" and "overwhelmed" consistently during that same period. Recognizing this connection helped her understand that both the headaches and emotional struggles were signs she needed additional support.

When to Reach Out:

Asking for help takes courage, not weakness. Mental health professionals are trained to help teenagers navigate exactly what they're experiencing. Consider reaching out when:

- Emotional struggles interfere with school, friendships, or family relationships
- You've tried self-care strategies for two weeks without improvement
- You are thinking of hurting yourself or others
- Substance use becomes a way to cope with emotions
- Friends or family complaining about changes they've

noticed

Resources Available to You:

- School counselors and nurses
- Your family doctor or pediatrician
- Mental health professionals who specialize in teenagers
- Crisis hotlines for immediate support
- Trusted family members or adult mentors

Remember that seeking help doesn't mean you're broken or weak. It means you're taking responsibility for your wellbeing and using all available resources to thrive.

Recap of Key Points

Your intense emotions are evidence of a developing brain, not a character flaw. Learning to name your feelings specifically using the mood wheel gives you power over them, while understanding your unique triggers helps you navigate challenging situations with intention. Most importantly, distinguishing between normal emotional difficulties and persistent struggles helps you know when to seek additional support—and there's strength in asking for help when you need it.

Action Steps

Start using the mood wheel this week whenever you notice powerful emotions—even positive ones. Keep a simple trigger tracker for three days, noting what situations or interactions consistently affect your mood. If you've been struggling for over two weeks with persistent sadness, low energy, or loss of interest in things you usually enjoy, consider talking to a trusted adult about getting professional support.

Now that you understand your emotions are normal and have tools to identify and track them, it's time to tackle one of the biggest emotional challenges teens face: that harsh inner voice that tells you you're not good enough. In the next chapter, we'll explore why you're so hard on yourself and learn strategies to transform self-criticism into self-compassion.

Chapter 2: The Inner Battle

Self-Doubt and Sensitivity

Silencing the Voice That Sabotages You

Picture this: You walk into first period and immediately notice your friend talking to someone else. Your brain instantly creates a story: "They're probably talking about how weird I was yesterday. I'm so annoying. No wonder they don't want to sit with me." Sound familiar? That voice in your head — the one that jumps to the worst plausible conclusion about everything you do is your inner critic, and it's working overtime during your teen years.

Remember from Chapter 1 how we talked about emotions being signals, not facts? Your inner critic is like a faulty smoke detector that goes off when you burn toast. It thinks it's protecting you from danger, but it's actually creating unnecessary panic.

Your inner critic develops from a mix of perfectionist expectations, social comparison, and your brain's natural tendency to focus on potential threats. Thanks, evolution. While this voice thinks it's protecting you from embarrassment or failure, it's actually creating more stress and keeping you stuck in cycles of self-doubt.

Understanding Your Inner Critic's Tactics

Your inner critic has some favorite tricks it uses to keep you feeling small:

- The Fortune Teller: It predicts the worst likely outcomes before anything even happens
- The Mind Reader: It insists it knows exactly what everyone else is thinking about you
- The Perfectionist: It sets impossible standards and then beats you up for not meeting them
- The Historian: It brings up every mistake you've ever made as evidence that you'll mess up again

The tricky part is that your inner critic sometimes sounds like it's being helpful. It might say things like, "I'm just trying to help you avoid mistakes," or, "I'm keeping you humble." But there's a big difference between helpful self-reflection and destructive self-attack.

The Expectations vs. Reality Gap

Your inner critic thrives on the distance between who you think you should be and who you are right now. It loves to point out every way you're falling short of some impossible standard. Maybe you think you should be naturally confident in every social situation, effortlessly smart in every class, or perfectly put-together all the time.

Here's the thing: those standards aren't realistic for anyone.

Even adults struggle with self-doubt and make mistakes daily. The difference is that many have learned to talk to themselves with more compassion.

The Mind Reading Trap

One of your inner critic's favorite games is convincing you that you know what others are thinking about you. Spoiler alert: you don't, and they're usually thinking about themselves anyway. When Evelyn walked into the cafeteria and saw people laughing, her inner critic immediately decided they were laughing at her outfit. In reality, her friend was telling a funny story about her cat getting stuck in a paper bag.

This mind-reading habit creates unnecessary stress and keeps you focused on imaginary problems instead of real ones.

Practical Strategies to Quiet the Critic

The Flip the Script Technique: When you catch your inner critic in action, try translating its harsh commentary into neutral, helpful facts. Instead of "I'm so stupid," try "I made a mistake and

I can learn from it." Instead of "Nobody likes me," try "I'm feeling left out right now, and that's uncomfortable."

Name Your Critic: Give your inner critic a name that takes away its power. Evelyn called hers "Dramatic Diana." Felix named his "Professor Pessimism." When you can recognize it as a separate voice rather than absolute truth, you can choose whether to listen to it.

The Evidence Game: When your inner critic makes a claim, ask for evidence. If it says, "You always mess everything up," challenge it to provide specific examples. Usually, it can't back up its extreme statements with facts.

Building Your Inner Supporter

While you're working on quieting your inner critic, start building a more supportive inner voice. This isn't about fake positivity or pretending problems don't exist. It's about treating yourself with the same kindness you'd show a good friend.

Practice talking to yourself like someone who cares about you and wants you to succeed. This supportive voice acknowledges challenges without attacking your worth as a person.

As we move into the next chapter about social media and comparison, remember that your inner critic loves to use other people's highlight reels as ammunition against you.

The goal isn't to eliminate self-reflection entirely.

It's to replace destructive self-attack with constructive self-awareness.

The Sensitivity Superpower Nobody Talks About

Maybe you've been told you're "too emotional," "too sensitive," or that you "take everything too personally." Maybe you've started believing it yourself. Here's the truth: sensitivity isn't a character flaw—it's actually a superpower that our society doesn't always know how to handle. When you feel deeply, you also love deeply, create beautifully, and understand others in ways that less sensitive people simply can't.

Remember from Chapter 1 when we talked about emotions being information rather than problems to fix? Your sensitivity is like having a high-definition emotional radar system. While others might miss the subtle signals in a room, you're picking up on everything—the tension in someone's voice, the way energy shifts when certain topics come up, the unspoken feelings floating beneath surface conversations.

Understanding Your Sensitivity

The myth that sensitivity equals weakness is just that—a myth. Research shows that highly sensitive people often become excellent leaders, artists, counselors, and innovators because they pick up on subtleties others miss. The problem isn't your sensitivity; it's learning how to manage it in a world that sometimes feels overwhelming.

About twenty percent of the population is born with a highly sensitive nervous system. This means your brain processes sensory information more thoroughly than others. You might notice:

- Background noises that others ignore
- Subtle changes in people's moods or energy
- Overwhelming feelings in crowded or chaotic environments
- Deep reactions to movies, books, or music
- Physical sensitivities to tags in clothing, bright lights, or powerful smells

None of these things are weaknesses.

They're simply how your nervous system is wired.

Sensitivity as Emotional Intelligence

Your ability to pick up on subtle mood changes, unspoken tensions, and emotional undercurrents is actually intelligence that many people lack. While others might walk into a room and miss the fact that two people just had an argument, you sense it immediately. This emotional awareness can feel overwhelming sometimes, but it also gives you incredible insight into human behavior and relationships.

Abigail realized her sensitivity was actually helping her friendships when she noticed her friend was struggling with her parents' divorce before anyone else did. While other friends kept wondering why their friend seemed distant, Abigail could offer support exactly when it was needed most. Her sensitivity allowed her to be the friend she wished she had.

Emotions influence how we think and respond.

The Creativity Connection

Many sensitive teens are also highly creative because they process experiences more deeply and notice details others overlook. Your rich inner world and emotional depth often translate into artistic expression, innovative problem-solving, or unique perspectives that others find valuable. Instead of seeing your intensity as something to tone down, consider it fuel for whatever creative outlets speak to you.

Managing Overwhelm Without Shutting Down

The challenge with sensitivity isn't the trait itself—it's learning to manage the overwhelm that can come with it. When everything feels intense, it's tempting to shut down emotionally or avoid situations altogether. But you don't have to choose between feeling everything or feeling nothing.

Create Emotional Boundaries: Just like physical boundaries protect your personal space, emotional boundaries protect your energy. You can care about people without absorbing their emotions as if they were your own.

The Energy Check-In: Before entering overwhelming situations, ask yourself: "What emotional energy am I bringing in, and what am I picking up from others?" This helps you distinguish between your feelings and everyone else's.

Recovery Time: Sensitive people need more downtime to process experiences and recharge. This isn't being antisocial—its necessary maintenance for your emotional well-being.

Boundary Scripts for Critics

When someone dismisses your feelings, try responses like, "My emotions are valid, even if you don't understand them," or "I'd rather feel too much than too little." You don't need to justify your emotional responses to people who don't understand sensitivity.

Alexander was constantly told by his family that he was "too dramatic" whenever he got upset about conflicts at home. He did not start believing something was wrong with him until his counselor pointed out that his sensitivity made him an incredible friend—he was the person everyone came to when they needed someone to really listen and understand. He learned to see his emotional depth as a gift rather than a burden and started surrounding himself with people who appreciated rather than criticized his caring nature.

Moving Forward with Your Superpower

As we move into discussing digital overwhelm in the next chapter, remember that sensitive people often feel social media more intensely than others. Your sensitivity isn't something to fix—it's something to understand and honor.

The goal is learning to thrive with your sensitivity, not despite it.

Chasing Perfect While Staying Sane

You know that feeling when you spend three hours on an assignment that should take 30 minutes because you keep rewriting the same paragraph? Or when you don't turn in a project at all because it's not "good enough" yet? Welcome to the perfectionist trap—where the pursuit of flawless work actually prevents you from doing any work at all.

Remember how we talked about your inner critic in the previous section? Perfectionism is often the critic's favorite weapon. It convinces you that anything less than perfect reflects poorly on your worth as a person, which makes every assignment feel like a test of your entire identity.

Understanding the Perfectionist Trap

Perfectionism isn't about having high standards; it's about having impossible standards that paralyze you with a fear of failure. The perfectionist mindset tricks you into believing that anything less than perfect is worthless, which makes starting and finishing projects feel terrifying.

Here's what perfectionism actually looks like in real life:

- Procrastinating on projects because you're afraid they won't be good enough
- Rewriting the same paragraph dozens of times
- Avoiding recent activities because you might not excel immediately
- Feeling crushed with disappointment over anything less than an A
- Comparing your behind-the-scenes struggles to other people's finished products

The irony of perfectionism is that it actually prevents you from achieving your goals. When you're so focused on avoiding mistakes, you often avoid taking action altogether.

The All-or-Nothing Thinking Pattern

Perfectionism thrives on black-and-white thinking. Your brain categorizes everything as either a complete success or a total failure, with no middle ground. This leaves no room for the messy, imperfect process of actual learning and growth.

Lucas struggled with this when learning guitar. He expected to play complex songs perfectly after just a few weeks of practice. When he made mistakes, he'd get so frustrated that he'd quit practicing for days. His guitar teacher finally helped him see that mistakes weren't failures—they were necessary steps in the learning process. Every wrong note was actually information about how to play better next time.

From Perfectionism to Progress-ism

The antidote to perfectionism isn't lowering your standards—it's changing what you measure. Instead of only celebrating perfect outcomes, start recognizing effort, improvement, and completion as valuable achievements.

Progress Over Perfection Tracking: Instead of only celebrating A+ outcomes, track effort, improvement, and completion. Did you start the project? Progress. Did you learn something new? Progress. Did you turn it in on time? Major progress.

The "Done is Better Than Perfect" Rule: Set a timer for tasks and commit to submitting whatever you have when time runs out. This trains your brain to prioritize completion over perfection.

The 80% Rule: Aim to complete tasks to about 80% of what you imagine perfect would look like. Most of the time, your 80% is actually much better than you think, and it's always better than 0% because you were too afraid to start.

Practical Anti-Perfectionist Strategies

Perfectionist Thought Interrupts: When you catch yourself thinking, "This has to be perfect," try replacing it with "This has to be " or "This has to be my best effort right now."

The Rough Draft Mindset: Approach every first attempt as a rough draft, not a final product. Give yourself permission to create something imperfect that you can improve later.

Time Boxing: set specific time limits for tasks and stick to them. When time's up, you're done, regardless of whether it feels perfect.

Mistake Reframing: Instead of seeing mistakes as evidence of failure, see them as data about what to adjust next time. Every mistake contains useful information.

Dorothy spent her entire junior year rewriting college application essays because nothing felt "good enough." She missed several deadlines and almost didn't apply to her dream school. Her mom finally sat her down and said, "A submitted B+ essay is infinitely better than a perfect essay that never gets sent." Dorothy learned to set "good enough" standards for herself—essays that were clear, honest, and well-written, but not necessarily literary masterpieces. She got into three of her top-choice schools with those "imperfect" essays.

Building Tolerance for Imperfection

Learning to tolerate imperfection is like building a muscle—it takes practice. Start with low-stakes situations where perfection doesn't matter much. Send a text without rereading it five times. Turn in homework that's complete but not polished. Wear an outfit that's good enough rather than perfect.

As we move into the next chapter about digital comparison, remember that social media feeds us a constant stream of other people's highlight reels, which can trigger perfectionist thinking.

The goal isn't to stop caring about quality.

It's to care more about progress than perfection.

Beyond the Lazy Label

If you've ever been called lazy for putting things off, let's set the record straight: procrastination usually has nothing to do with laziness and everything to do with fear, overwhelm, or perfectionism. When your brain perceives a task as threatening (whether it's fear of failure, fear of success, or just feeling overwhelmed by where to start), it activates your fight-or-flight response. Since you can't fight or run away from homework, your brain chooses option three: freeze.

Remember from Chapter 1 how we talked about emotions being signals that give us important information? Procrastination is your brain's way of signaling that something about the task feels unsafe or overwhelming. Just like your inner critic from earlier in this chapter, procrastination thinks it's protecting you from potential pain or embarrassment.

The Real Reason Behind Procrastination

Understanding the actual reason behind procrastination is the first step to overcoming it. Most of the time, you're not avoiding work because you're lazy—you're avoiding the uncomfortable feelings that come with the work. Once you identify what you're really avoiding (judgment, failure, overwhelm), you can address the root cause instead of just forcing yourself to "try harder."

Fear-Based Delays: Often we put things off because we're afraid of doing them poorly, being judged, or discovering we're not as capable as we hoped. Recognizing these fears helps you address them directly.

Perfectionist Paralysis: earlier, when you believe something has to be perfect, starting becomes terrifying because you know it won't be perfect right away.

Overwhelm Shutdown: Sometimes tasks feel so big or complex that your brain literally doesn't know where to begin, so it shuts down instead.

Success Avoidance: Believe it or not, some people procrastinate because they're afraid of succeeding. Success can bring new expectations and responsibilities that feel scary.

Practical Anti-Procrastination Strategies

The "2-Minute Rule": If something takes less than two minutes, do it immediately. For bigger tasks, commit to just two minutes of work—often starting is the hardest part, and momentum will carry you forward.

Task Chunking: Break large projects into smaller, specific steps. Instead of "write history paper," try "choose topic," then "find three sources," then "write outline." Smaller steps feel less overwhelming and give you more opportunities to feel accomplished.

The Terrible First Draft Method: Give yourself permission to create something awful just to get started. You can't edit a blank page, but you can always improve a terrible first draft.

Environment Design: Set up your space to make starting easier and avoiding harder. Put your phone in another room, have your materials ready, and eliminate obvious distractions.

Compassionate Productivity: Instead of beating yourself up for procrastinating (which just creates more negative emotions to avoid), practice self-forgiveness and gentle redirection: "I got off track, and that's human. What's one small thing I can do right now?"

Lucas thought he was just lazy because he could never seem to start his history papers until the night before they were due. When he talked to his school counselor, he realized he was actually terrified of writing something stupid and having his teacher think he wasn't smart. Once he understood that fear was driving his procrastination, he started using the "terrible first draft" method—giving himself permission to write badly just to get started. Knowing he could always revise later made it much easier to begin, and his grades improved dramatically.

Recap of Key Points

The inner battles you face—self-doubt, sensitivity, perfectionism, and procrastination—aren't character flaws or signs that something is wrong with you. Your inner critic is trying to protect you but often creates more problems than it solves. Your sensitivity is actually a strength that allows you to connect deeply with others and create meaningful work. Perfectionism might seem like it's helping you achieve more, but it often prevents you from achieving anything at all. And procrastination usually stems from fear or overwhelm, not laziness. Understanding the real root of these struggles gives you the power to address them with compassion and practical strategies.

Action Steps

- Name your inner critic and practice the "flip the script" technique when you catch it being harsh
- Write down three ways your sensitivity has been a strength or gift in your life
- Choose one project or task where you can practice "good enough" standards instead of perfectionism
- Identify what emotion you're really avoiding the next time you find yourself procrastinating
- Practice the 2-minute rule for minor tasks this week

Now that we've tackled the internal battles happening in your mind, it's time to address the external pressures that can amplify these struggles. In our hyper-connected world, social media and digital spaces create new challenges around comparison, FOMO, and managing your online presence. Chapter 3 will give you the tools to navigate the digital world without losing yourself in the highlight reel of others' lives.

Chapter 3: The Digital World

Comparison and FOMO

When Perfect Lives Become Your Prison

It's 10 PM and you're lying in bed, mindlessly scrolling through Instagram. Everyone looks perfect—flawless skin, amazing vacations, friend groups that seem straight out of a movie. By the time you put your phone down, you feel like garbage about your own life.

Sound familiar?

Social media shows us everyone's highlight reel, not their behind-the-scenes reality. What you're seeing is carefully curated, filtered, and edited to look perfect. It's like comparing your rough draft to someone else's final published book—it's not a fair comparison, and it's definitely not the whole story.

Remember from Chapter 2 how we talked about that inner voice that tells you you're not enough? Social media feeds that voice like adding gasoline to a fire. The same sensitivity that makes you deeply aware of others' emotions also makes you more susceptible to comparison triggers online.

The Hidden Truth About Social Feeds

Every post you see went through a selection process. People don't share photos of their messy bedrooms, failed tests, or family arguments. They don't post about feeling lonely on Saturday night or struggling with anxiety before school.

Here's what really happens behind those perfect posts:

- The curation illusion: People post their best moments, not their mundane Tuesday afternoons or mental health struggles
- Filter reality distortion: Apps and filters create impossible beauty standards that don't exist in real life
- The mood tracking connection: Most people feel worse about themselves after extended social media use, but we rarely notice the pattern

The algorithms make this worse by showing you content that keeps you scrolling, which often means showing you things that trigger strong emotions—including envy and inadequacy.

Breaking Down FOMO

Fear of Missing Out isn't just about parties you weren't invited to. It's about feeling like everyone else is living a better, more exciting life than you are. FOMO triggers the same stress response in your brain as real physical danger.

When you see posts of friends hanging out without you, your nervous system doesn't know the difference between being left out and being in actual peril. Your heart races, your breathing gets shallow, and that familiar knot forms in your stomach.

This connects directly to the emotional sensitivity we explored in the previous chapter. If you're already prone to feeling things deeply, FOMO hits even harder.

Grace used to spend hours on TikTok every night before bed. She noticed she always felt anxious and inadequate afterward, comparing her regular teenage life to the seemingly perfect lives of influencers. When she started tracking her mood before and after scrolling (rating herself 1-10 on how good she felt), she discovered a clear pattern: she consistently felt 2-3 points worse after social media sessions. This simple awareness helped her recognize when she was falling into the comparison trap.

The Real Cost of Digital Comparison

Constant comparison doesn't just make you feel bad in the moment. It rewires your brain to focus on what you lack instead of what you have. Over time, this creates a persistent sense of inadequacy that follows you offline too.

You might find yourself:

- Questioning your appearance more often

- Feeling disconnected from real-life friendships
- Struggling to enjoy the present moments because you're thinking about what would look good online
- Developing unrealistic expectations for your own life

Creating Healthy Digital Boundaries

The goal isn't to delete all social media apps and live like it's 1995. The goal is to use these platforms intentionally instead of letting them use you.

Start by paying attention to how different accounts make you feel. Unfollow accounts that consistently trigger comparison or negative self-talk. Follow accounts that inspire you or make you laugh instead.

Set specific times for checking social media rather than mindlessly scrolling throughout the day. Notice when you're using your phone to avoid uncomfortable feelings—this awareness alone can break automatic scrolling habits.

Most importantly, remember that your worth isn't measured in likes, follows, or how your life stacks up against someone's carefully crafted online presence.

Your real life, with all its ordinary moments and imperfections, has value that no filter can capture.

In our next chapter, we'll tackle another major source of comparison and stress: school. Academic pressure can trigger many of the same emotional patterns we've been discussing, but with strategies tailored for classroom challenges.

Breaking Free from Comparison's Grip

Your stomach drops. Your heart races. You see a post of your friends hanging out without you, or someone your age achieving something incredible, and suddenly you feel you're failing at life. Your body is trying to tell you something: you've entered the comparison spiral.

The comparison spiral happens when we see something online that triggers our insecurities, and our minds start racing with "Why not me?" thoughts. The good news? Your body gives you warning signs before your thoughts completely take over, and you can learn to catch yourself in the act.

Recognizing Your Early Warning System

Remember from Chapter 1 how we talked about emotions being messengers? Your body's physical reactions to comparison are like a smoke detector going off before the fire spreads. These signals appear seconds before your thoughts spiral out of control.

Learning to notice these early warning signs is crucial because once the spiral fully starts, it's much harder to stop. Think of it like catching a small snowball before it becomes an avalanche.

Your nervous system doesn't distinguish between seeing a perfect Instagram post and facing a real threat. Both trigger the same fight-or-flight response we discussed in previous chapters. This is why comparison feels so intense physically—your body thinks you're in actual danger.

Common physical warning signs include:

- Physical warning signs: Stomach dropping, heart racing, tension in shoulders, or sudden restlessness
- The "interrupt" technique: Naming what's happening ("I'm comparing myself right now") to break the automatic pattern
- Rapid reset methods: Closing the app immediately, taking three deep breaths, or physically moving to a different location

The Power of the Interrupt

Once you recognize your warning signs, you have a critical window of opportunity. This is where the "interrupt" technique comes in—consciously stopping the automatic pattern before it takes over.

The moment you notice those physical sensations, say out loud or in your head: "I'm comparing myself right now." This simple acknowledgment interrupts the automatic response and gives your prefrontal cortex (the thinking part of your brain) a chance to take back control.

It might seem too simple to work, but naming what's happening activates the rational part of your brain that can make better choices. Without this interrupt, you'll likely continue scrolling and feeling worse.

Ian noticed that whenever he saw posts about college acceptances or academic achievements, his chest would get tight and he'd start spiraling into thoughts about not being smart enough. He learned to recognize that physical tightness as his "comparison alarm." Now when he feels it, he immediately closes the app and does 10 pushups to reset his energy. This simple physical interrupt stops the spiral before it takes over his whole day.

Quick Reset Strategies

After you interrupt the pattern, you need a reset strategy to shift your emotional state. The key is having these strategies ready before you need them, like having a fire extinguisher before there's a fire.

Physical resets work particularly well because they help discharge the stress energy your body created. Try jumping jacks, pushups, or even just standing up and stretching. Movement tells your nervous system that you're safe and the "threat" has passed.

Environmental resets involve changing your physical space. Put your phone in another room, go outside, or move to a different part of your house. This physical shift helps break the mental loop.

Grounding resets bring you back to the present moment. Look around and name five things you can see, four things you can touch, three things you can hear, two things you can smell, and one thing you can taste.

Building Your Comparison Immunity

The more you practice these interrupt and reset techniques, the stronger your "comparison immunity" becomes. You'll start catching yourself earlier and recovering faster when comparison thoughts arise.

This connects to the emotional sensitivity we explored in Chapter 2. If you're naturally sensitive, you might feel comparison triggers more intensely, but you can also develop stronger awareness of your warning signs.

The goal isn't to never feel comparison again—that's impossible. The goal is to recognize it quickly and choose your response instead of letting it choose for you.

As we move into the next chapter about school stress, you'll notice how these same patterns show up in academic settings. The pressure to perform and compete with classmates can trigger similar comparison spirals, but with the tools you're learning, you'll be ready to handle them.

Breaking Free from the Sidelines

You open Snapchat and see story after story from the party you weren't invited to. Everyone looks like they're having the time of their lives, and you're sitting at home in your pajamas feeling like a complete loser. The fear of missing out (FOMO) can make exclusion feel like social death.

Here's what most people don't know: exclusion actually activates the same pain centers in your brain as physical injury. Your brain literally processes being left out as a threat to your survival. No wonder it hurts so much! Understanding this can help you be gentler with yourself when FOMO hits hard.

Why FOMO Feels Like Physical Pain

Think back to Chapter 1 where we talked about emotions being messengers. FOMO is your brain's ancient alarm system screaming that your social survival might be at risk. Thousands of years ago, being excluded from the tribe could literally mean death, so your nervous system treats social exclusion as a genuine emergency.

This connects directly to the emotional sensitivity we explored in Chapter 2. If you're naturally more attuned to social cues and relationships, exclusion hits even harder because your brain processes social information more intensely.

The same fight-or-flight response that gets triggered by physical danger kicks in when you see evidence that you've been left out. Your heart races, your stomach churns, and your thoughts spiral into worst-case scenarios about what this means for your friendships.

The Stories We Tell Ourselves

When FOMO strikes, your mind immediately starts creating explanations for why you weren't included. Unfortunately, these explanations are usually the worst possible interpretations of the situation.

Your brain fills in missing information with fears:

- "They don't really like me"
- "I'm not fun enough to invite"
- "They were talking about me and decided I shouldn't come"

- "This proves I don't really belong in this group"

But here's the reality: you don't have the full story. You don't know who made the guest list, what the limitations were, or what factors influenced the invitation decisions. Social media shows you the event, but it doesn't show you the context.

Reframing the Narrative

When FOMO hits, you need tools to challenge those automatic negative thoughts before they spiral out of control. This is where perspective reframes come in—alternative ways of interpreting the situation that are more balanced and realistic.

Useful perspective reframes include:

- The science of social pain: Exclusion triggers real pain responses in your brain, so the hurt you feel is legitimate
- Perspective reframes: "Not being included in this one thing doesn't mean I'm not valued" and "I don't know the full story behind why I wasn't invited"
- Immediate coping strategies: Reaching out to one person who cares about you, doing something kind for yourself, or engaging in an activity that makes you feel competent

These reframes don't eliminate the hurt, but they prevent you from making the situation worse by adding layers of self-criticism and catastrophic thinking on top of the natural disappointment.

Moving from Reaction to Response

Remember the difference between reacting and responding from our earlier chapters? FOMO typically triggers immediate reactions—checking social media obsessively, sending desperate texts to friends, or withdrawing completely from social situations.

A thoughtful response involves pausing, acknowledging the hurt, and choosing actions that actually make you feel better rather than worse.

Mary saw Instagram stories from a birthday party she wasn't invited to and spent the whole weekend convinced she was being intentionally excluded by her friend group. She later found out the party was limited to family friends only because of the parents' rules, but by then she'd already made herself miserable with worst-case-scenario thinking. Now when she sees posts that trigger FOMO, she waits 24 hours before drawing any conclusions about what it means for her friendships.

Immediate Coping Strategies

When FOMO hits hard, you need immediate tools to help yourself feel better in the moment. The goal isn't to pretend you don't care—it's to take care of yourself while you're hurting.

Try reaching out to one person who you know cares about you. This doesn't mean complaining about being excluded; it means connecting with someone who reminds you that you matter.

Do something kind for yourself. Take a warm shower, make your favorite snack, or watch something that makes you laugh. Treat yourself the way you'd treat a good friend who was feeling hurt.

Engage in an activity that makes you feel competent and valuable. Work on a hobby you're good at, help someone with something, or do any activity where you feel skilled and useful.

As we move into our next chapter about school stress, you'll see how these same social comparison patterns show up in academic settings. The pressure to measure up to classmates and meet expectations can trigger similar emotional spirals, but you'll have the tools to handle them.

Breaking Free from Screen Addiction

What if you could remember what it feels like to be bored? To sit with your thoughts without immediately reaching for your phone? To have a conversation without checking notifications? A digital detox isn't about demonizing technology—it's about remembering that you have a choice in how you engage with it.

Taking intentional breaks from social media and digital stimulation can reset your nervous system, improve your sleep, and help you reconnect with activities that actually energize you instead of draining you. Even a 24-hour break can give you valuable insights about your relationship with technology.

Why Your Brain Craves Digital Stimulation

Remember from Chapter 1 how we talked about emotions being messengers? Your phone has hijacked your brain's reward system, creating artificial emotional highs and lows that keep you coming back for more. Every notification triggers a small hit of dopamine—the same neurotransmitter involved in addiction.

This connects to the sensitivity we explored in Chapter 2. If you're naturally more emotionally responsive, you might be even more susceptible to the emotional roller coaster that social media creates. Your nervous system gets stuck in a cycle of artificial stimulation and subsequent crashes.

Your brain starts to crave this constant input, making it harder to tolerate normal moments of quiet or boredom. But boredom isn't the enemy—it's actually when your brain does some of its most important work, like processing emotions and making creative connections.

The Benefits of Stepping Away

Digital detoxes aren't punishment; they're reset buttons for your emotional system. When you step away from screens, several important things happen:

Your sleep improves because you're not exposing your brain to blue light and emotional stimulation right before bed. Your attention span increases because you're not constantly switching between tasks and notifications.

Most importantly, you start to notice how you actually feel without the artificial emotional highs and lows of social media. Many people discover they feel calmer, more creative, and more connected to the people physically around them.

Starting Your Digital Detox

The key to a successful digital detox is starting small and building gradually. Going from checking your phone 200 times a day to zero overnight is like trying to run a marathon without training—you'll probably give up quickly.

- Start small: Begin with phone-free meals or the first hour after waking up, then gradually extend the time
- Create physical barriers: Put your phone in another room, use app timers, or give your phone to a family member during detox hours
- Build an "offline menu": Prepare a list of activities you enjoy that don't involve screens—reading, drawing, walking, cooking, or calling a friend

Physical barriers are crucial because willpower alone isn't enough when you're breaking a habit. If your phone is within arm's reach, you'll probably check it out of automatic response, even during your detox time.

What to Expect During Your Detox

The first few hours might feel uncomfortable. You'll probably reach for your phone out of habit multiple times. This is normal and doesn't mean you're failing. Your brain is simply looking for its usual source of stimulation.

You might feel restless or even slightly anxious at first. This is your nervous system adjusting to the absence of constant digital input. Push through this initial discomfort—it usually passes within a few hours.

Eric realized he was checking his phone over 200 times per day and felt constantly anxious. He decided to try a weekend digital detox, giving his phone to his mom on Friday night and getting it back Sunday evening. The first few hours were uncomfortable—he kept reaching for his phone out of habit. But by Saturday afternoon, he noticed he felt calmer and more present. He spent time reading a book he'd been meaning to finish and had an actual conversation with his dad about music. The experience showed him how much mental space his phone had been occupying.

Creating Sustainable Digital Habits

The goal isn't to never use social media again. The goal is to use it intentionally rather than compulsively. After your detox experience, you'll have better awareness of when you're using technology as a genuine tool versus when you're using it to avoid uncomfortable feelings.

You might discover that checking social media first thing in the morning sets a comparison tone for your whole day, or that scrolling before bed makes it harder to fall asleep. These insights help you create personalized boundaries that work for your life.

Recap of Key Points

Social media shows us highlight reels, not reality, and comparing our behind-the-scenes to others' curated content is a recipe for feeling inadequate. Your body gives you warning signs when you're entering a comparison spiral—learn to recognize and interrupt these moments. FOMO and exclusion cause real emotional pain, but one social situation doesn't define your worth or your relationships. Taking intentional breaks from digital stimulation can help you reconnect with yourself and activities that truly energize you.

Action Steps

This week, try the "scroll audit"—rate your mood before and after using social media to notice patterns. Practice the physical interrupt technique when you feel comparison starting. Create your personal "offline menu" with 10 activities you can do instead of scrolling. Consider trying a mini digital detox, even if it's just for a few hours.

Now that we've tackled the digital world's impact on your emotional well-being, let's dive into another major source of stress for most teens: school. From test anxiety to homework overwhelm to dealing with difficult teachers, Chapter 4 will give you practical tools for surviving and thriving in academic environments.

Chapter 4: School Survival- Stress, Tests, and Grades

When Sleep Meets Racing Thoughts

It's 11:47 PM. You're lying in bed, eyes closed, but your brain is hosting a full-blown conference about tomorrow's presentation, that awkward thing you said in third period, and whether you remembered to charge your phone. Sound familiar? Your mind isn't broken—it's just processing the day when everything finally gets quiet.

When your head hits the pillow, your brain often kicks into overdrive because it's finally free from distractions. The stress hormone cortisol can spike at night, especially when you're worried about school performance. This creates a cruel cycle: the more you worry about not sleeping, the more awake you become.

Remember how we talked about digital comparison in Chapter 3? That late-night scroll through social media doesn't just feed FOMO—it also disrupts your natural sleep rhythm. Your brain sees those blue-lit screens and thinks it's daytime, keeping you wired when you should wind down.

The Science Behind Racing Thoughts

Your brain processes about 70,000 thoughts per day. During busy school periods, many of these thoughts center on performance, deadlines, and social situations. When you finally lie down, your prefrontal cortex—the part responsible for decision-making and worry—doesn't automatically shut off. It keeps reviewing the day and planning for tomorrow.

Sleep is when your brain merges memories and processes emotions from the day. But if you're flooded with stress hormones from academic pressure, this natural process gets hijacked. Instead of peaceful rest, you get mental replay after mental replay.

Practical Strategies for Calmer Nights

The "knowledge transfer" Strategy: keep a notebook by your bed and write every worry, task, or random thought for 5-10 minutes. This signals to your brain that these concerns are "saved" and don't need to loop endlessly. Helen discovered this technique during finals week. She wrote three pages of jumbled thoughts and worries, then slept for eight straight hours—her best sleep in weeks.

The "3-2-1 Wind Down": Three hours before bed, no more enormous meals. Two hours before, no more homework or intense conversations. One hour before, no more screens. This gives your nervous system time to shift into rest mode. Think of it as creating a buffer zone between your day brain and your sleep brain.

Progressive Muscle Relaxation: Starting with your toes, tense each muscle group for five seconds, then release. Work your way up to your head. This technique tricks your body into recognizing the difference between tension and relaxation.

When Worry Wakes You Up

Sometimes you'll fall asleep fine but wake up at 2 AM with your heart racing about that test you forgot to study for. This is normal, but it doesn't have to ruin your night.

The "Sleep SOS Protocol": If you wake up panicking at 3 AM, don't check your phone. The blue light will convince your brain it's morning time. Instead, practice the "4-7-8" breathing technique: inhale for 4 counts, hold for 7, exhale for 8. Repeat until your heart rate slows.

The "Worry Window": Set aside 15 minutes during the day specifically for worrying about school stuff. When nighttime worries pop up, remind yourself: "I'll think about this during my worry window tomorrow."

Building Better Sleep Habits

Your sleep affects everything—your mood, focus, memory, and ability to handle stress. When you're well-rested, the triggers we discussed in earlier chapters feel more manageable. Poor sleep makes even minor problems feel huge.

Create a consistent bedtime routine that signals to your brain it's time to wind down. This might include reading, gentle stretching, or listening to calm music. Felix started doing five minutes of journaling every night, writing down three things that went well that day. His racing thoughts gradually shifted from problems to positive moments.

Quality sleep isn't a luxury—it's essential for emotional regulation. When you prioritize rest, you're building a foundation that makes everything else in school feel more manageable.

Tomorrow, we'll explore what happens when emotions get really intense and drama brews. But for tonight, your job is simple: rest well.

Beat Test Anxiety in One Minute

Your palms are sweating, your heart is pounding, and you can't remember your own name, let alone the answer to question three. Test anxiety is your brain's alarm system going off when there's no genuine emergency—just a piece of paper that feels like it determines your entire future.

Performance anxiety is completely normal and affects even the most prepared students. Your sympathetic nervous system activates the same fight-or-flight response whether you're facing a tiger or a calculus exam. The good news? You can hack this system with quick, desk-friendly techniques that work in under a minute.

Remember from Chapter 1 how we talked about emotions being messengers? Test anxiety is your brain's way of saying, "This matters to you." The problem isn't the caring—it's when that caring hijacks your ability to think clearly. Just like the digital overwhelm we discussed in Chapter 3, test anxiety floods your system with more input than you can process effectively.

The Physical Side of Panic

When you sit down for a test, your amygdala—the brain's alarm center—scans for threats. Even though a math quiz isn't actually dangerous, your brain treats academic performance like survival. This triggers a cascade of stress hormones that makes your heart race, your hands shake, and your mind go blank.

Your body is literally preparing to run from danger when what you need is to sit still and think. This mismatch between what your body wants to do and what you need to do creates even more anxiety.

Quick Reset Techniques

Box Breathing (4-4-4-4): Inhale for 4 counts, hold for 4, exhale for 4, hold empty for 4. This activates your parasympathetic nervous system, telling your body it's safe to think clearly again. You can do this silently at your desk without anyone noticing.

The "5-4-3-2-1 Grounding": Name 5 things you can see, 4 you can touch, 3 you can hear, 2 you can smell, 1 you can taste. This pulls your attention away from panic and into the present moment. Your pen, the desk texture, classroom sounds—use whatever is around you.

Progressive Muscle Relaxation: Tense your shoulders for 5 seconds, then release. Do the same with your hands, jaw, and feet. This releases physical tension blocks clear thinking. You can do this subtly without drawing attention.

Mental Tricks That Actually Work

The "Good Enough" Mindset: Perfectionism fuels test anxiety. Remind yourself that you don't need to ace every question to succeed. Sometimes "good enough" really is good enough. This takes pressure off and allows your actual knowledge to surface.

Question Triage: Scan the entire test first and tackle easier questions. This builds confidence and momentum while giving your brain time to work on harder problems in the background. Success breeds success, even in small doses.

The "Teaching" Method: When you hit a difficult question, imagine explaining the concept to a friend. This shifts your brain from panic mode into explanation mode, which often unlocks the information you need.

Real Student Success Stories

Edward discovered his test anxiety was worst during the first five minutes of any exam. He started using the box breathing technique as soon as he sat down, before even looking at the questions. "It's like hitting a reset button," he says. His grades improved not because he studied more, but because his mind was calm enough to access what he already knew.

Violet used to freeze completely during timed tests. She learned to do a quick body scan—noticing where she held tension and consciously relaxing those muscles. This simple awareness helped her stay present instead of spiraling into panic.

Building Long-Term Confidence

Quick techniques help in the moment, but building lasting confidence requires changing how you think about tests. Instead of viewing them as judgment of your worth, see them as chances to show what you've learned. This shift takes time, but it transforms your entire relationship with academic pressure.

These skills prepare you for the next chapter, where we'll explore what happens when emotions get really intense. The same techniques that calm test anxiety also help when anger and drama heat up.

Your worth isn't determined by a grade. Period.

Drowning in Homework Mountain Rescue

You open your planner and see: math homework, history essay, science lab report, college application, and somehow you're supposed to respond to seventeen group chats. The list feels infinite, and you haven't even started. This is when your brain screams "RUN!" and you end up scrolling TikTok instead of tackling anything.

Overwhelm isn't about having too much to do—it's about your brain's inability to process multiple large tasks simultaneously. When everything feels equally urgent and important, your executive function shuts down. The solution isn't working harder; it's working smarter by breaking the avalanche into manageable snowballs.

Remember from Chapter 2 how we discussed the inner critic that tells you you're not good enough? That voice gets louder when you're drowning in work. And just like the FOMO spiral we explored in Chapter 3, academic overwhelm feeds on itself—the more behind you feel, the more paralyzed you become.

Why Your Brain Freezes

When faced with multiple big tasks, your prefrontal cortex—the brain's CEO—gets overloaded trying to process everything at once. It's like having too many browser tabs open on an old computer. Eventually, the whole system crashes, and you can't function at all.

Your brain literally can't prioritize when everything feels like a crisis. This triggers your stress response, flooding your system with cortisol and adrenaline. These chemicals are great for running from danger but terrible for sitting down to write an essay.

The Micro-Chunking Revolution

Micro-Chunking Method: Take any large assignment and break it into 10-15 minute tasks. Instead of "write history essay," try "find three sources," then "write thesis statement," then "outline intro paragraph." Your brain can handle small, specific actions.

The key is making tasks so small they feel almost silly to avoid. "Open Google Docs" is easier to start than "write five-page research paper." Once you begin the tiny task, momentum often carries you further than you planned.

The "Done Jar" System: Write each micro-task on a slip of paper. When you complete it, put the paper in a jar. Watching the jar fill up gives you visual proof of progress, even when the big project isn't finished yet. This satisfies your brain's need for immediate rewards while working toward long-term goals.

Smart Prioritization Strategies

Priority Triage: Use the "Must, Should, Could" system. Must = due tomorrow and affects your grade. Should = important but has some flexibility. Could be nice but won't derail your life if postponed.

The "Two-Minute Rule": If something takes less than two minutes, do it immediately. Reply to that email, organize your desk, or review tomorrow's schedule. This prevents minor tasks from piling up into an overwhelming mountain.

Energy Matching: Match your most challenging work to your peak energy times. If you're sharpest in the morning, tackle difficult subjects then. Save routine tasks like organizing notes for when you're tired.

Real Success Stories

Lauren was drowning in AP coursework and felt like she was failing at everything. She started using the micro-chunking method, setting a timer for 15-minute work sprints with 5-minute breaks. "I realized I wasn't lazy," she reflected. "I was just overwhelmed by how big everything seemed. Breaking it down made it feel possible again." She went from chronic procrastination to completing assignments early.

Aiden discovered that his overwhelm peaked on Sunday nights when he looked at the week ahead. He started doing a "Sunday Setup"—spending twenty minutes breaking the week's big tasks into daily micro-chunks. This simple planning session transformed his Monday mornings from panic to purpose.

Building Sustainable Habits

The goal isn't to become a productivity machine. It's to develop systems that work with your brain instead of against it. When you feel that familiar overwhelm creeping in, remember: you don't have to climb the entire mountain today. You just need to take the next step.

These organizational skills become even more important when emotions run high. In our next chapter, we'll explore what happens when overwhelm meets anger, and how to cool down the heat before it burns everything down.

Your to-do list doesn't define your worth. Progress beats perfection every single time.

Bridging the Gap with Educators

You're struggling in chemistry, but the thought of asking for help makes your stomach twist. What if your teacher thinks you're making excuses? What if they say you should have asked sooner?

What if they're too busy to care? So you suffer in silence, watching your grade slip further into the danger zone.

Many teens avoid reaching out to teachers because they fear being judged as lazy, dramatic, or incapable. But most teachers became educators because they want to help students succeed. The key is approaching them with a clear request and a collaborative attitude, not a list of excuses.

Remember from Chapter 2 how we talked about the inner critic that assumes the worst about how others see you? That same voice whispers that teachers will think less of you for needing help. And just like the comparison trap we explored in Chapter 3, you might assume everyone else understands the material perfectly while you're the only one struggling.

Why Teacher Conversations Feel Scary

Your brain treats academic failure as a threat to your social standing and future security. When you're behind in a class, approaching the teacher activates the same fear response as approaching someone you have a crush on—your nervous system can't tell the difference between social rejection and actual danger.

Add to this the power imbalance between students and teachers, and it's no wonder these conversations feel intimidating. You're essentially admitting vulnerability to someone who has authority over your grades and daily experience.

Smart Communication Strategies

Prep Your Main Point: Before the conversation, write exactly what you need. "I'm struggling with balancing equations and need help to understand the steps" is much more effective than "Chemistry is really hard." Specific requests get specific help.

Time It Right: Don't corner your teacher thirty seconds before class starts or immediately after they've dealt with a classroom crisis. Email to schedule a brief meeting or arrive early when they're setting up for the day. Timing shows respect for their schedules.

Use "I" Statements: "I'm having trouble keeping up with the pace" sounds more responsible than "You're going too fast." This frames the conversation as problem-solving rather than blame. Teachers respond much better when they don't feel attacked.

Suggest Solutions: Come with ideas, not just problems. "Could I get the notes from yesterday's class?" or "Would it help if I came to office hours twice a week?" shows you're willing to put in the effort. Teachers want to help students who help themselves.

Breaking Down the Conversation

Start with appreciation: "Thanks for taking the time to talk with me." Then state your challenge clearly: "I'm struggling with the essay structure in this class." Follow with a specific request: "Could you look at my outline and give me feedback?" End with a commitment: "I'll revise it and check back with you next week."

This structure shows respect, clarity, and responsibility. It's much more effective than vague complaints or emotional appeals.

Real Student Breakthroughs

Jacob was failing English because he couldn't keep up with the reading assignments because of his dyslexia, but he was too embarrassed to explain his learning difference. Finally, he scheduled a meeting and said, "I'm struggling to finish the readings on time because of my dyslexia. Could we discuss some accommodations?" His teacher immediately offered audiobook versions and extended deadlines. "I wasted months suffering when the solution was one conversation away," he realized.

Sarah thought her math teacher hated her because she never understood the material. When she finally asked for help, she discovered her teacher had been waiting all semester for students to come to office hours. "I thought asking for help meant I was dumb," Sarah says. "But she told me that the smartest students are the ones who ask questions."

Building Ongoing Relationships

One positive interaction often opens the door to ongoing support. Teachers notice when students take initiative to improve, and they're more likely to offer extra help, extensions, or encouragement to students who communicate proactively.

Teachers are human beings who chose a profession focused on helping young people learn and grow. Most of them genuinely want you to succeed and will work with you if you give them the chance.

These communication skills become even more important when emotions run high. In our next chapter, we'll explore what happens when the pressure cooker of daily life causes you to explode at the people you care about most.

Chapter 5: Anger and Drama

Cooling Down the Heat

When Home Becomes a Battlefield

Picture this: You walk through the door after a brutal day at school dealing with test stress and academic pressure like we talked about in the last chapter, and your mom immediately asks why you didn't respond to her texts. Your dad chimes in about the dishes in the sink. Your little brother is being loud, and suddenly you're yelling at everyone like you just lost your mind. Five minutes later, you're in your room wondering why you exploded over something so small.

Sound familiar?

Home drama hits differently because these are the people who see you at your worst. They're supposed to be your safe space, but sometimes family becomes the place where all your built-up emotions from school and life finally burst out like a shaken soda can.

Understanding Your Anger Blueprint

Anger rarely shows up alone—it's usually the bodyguard for other emotions like hurt, frustration, or feeling overwhelmed. When we understand what's really driving our anger, we can catch it before it takes the wheel and crashes into everyone we care about.

Think of anger as an iceberg floating in cold water. What you see on the surface might yell, slamming doors, or giving people the silent treatment. But underneath that visible anger are all the genuine emotions that need attention:

- Exhaustion from juggling too many responsibilities
- Disappointment when expectations don't match reality
- Hurt feelings result when someone says something careless
- Feeling unheard when your perspective gets dismissed
- Overwhelmed from having too much on your plate

The key is learning to identify what's beneath your anger before it explodes everywhere.

The Traffic Light System

Here's a simple way to catch your anger before it causes damage. Imagine your emotional state like a traffic light:

Green Light = Calm

You feel relaxed, your body is loose, and you can think clearly about problems.

Yellow Light = Tension Building

Your jaw gets tight, thoughts race, you feel heat in your chest, or you notice yourself getting annoyed at small things. This is your warning signal.

Red Light = About to Explode

Your heart is pounding, you feel like you might say something you'll regret, and rational thinking has left the building.

The goal isn't to never feel angry. The goal is catching yourself at yellow and using some tools to cool down before you hit red.

Common Home Triggers

Family anger often stems from predictable situations. See if any of these sound like your house:

- Feeling controlled when parents micromanage your choices
- Being interrupted when you're trying to explain something important
- Privacy invasion when siblings go through your stuff without asking

- Unfair comparisons to brothers, sisters, or cousins who seem perfect
- Timing clashes when family wants attention but you need space
- Miscommunication when people assume they know what you're thinking

Keira had been getting snappy with her parents every evening for weeks. When she started tracking her yellow-light moments, she realized they always happened right after school when she was mentally drained but her family wanted to immediately connect. She learned to say, "I need twenty minutes to decompress, then I want to hear about your day too." This simple boundary prevented most of her explosions and actually improved her relationships at home.

The Cool-Down Toolkit

When you notice yourself hitting yellow, try these quick strategies:

- Take five deep breaths and count them slowly
- Step outside for a few minutes of fresh air
- Listen to one song that helps you feel calmer
- Write down what's really bothering you underneath the anger
- Do jumping jacks or push-ups to burn off physical tension

Cooling down isn't about stuffing your feelings or pretending everything is fine. It's about getting yourself to a place where you can address the real issues without burning down your relationships.

When Friends Clash, Choose Your Move

Your best friend just posted a story with people you thought didn't like her, and she's been "too busy" to hang out with you for weeks. Your fingers are already typing a passive-aggressive comment when you catch yourself. This is the moment that determines whether you're responding thoughtfully or reacting on emotional autopilot.

Just like we learned to catch our anger before it explodes at home, friendship conflicts need the same yellow-light awareness we talked about in the previous section.

The React vs. Respond Choice

The difference between responding and reacting can save friendships. Reacting is immediate and emotional—it feels good in the moment but usually makes things worse. Responding takes a beat to consider what you actually want to accomplish and how to get there without burning bridges.

Reacting looks like:

- Firing off angry texts without thinking
- Making cutting comments designed to hurt
- Giving someone the silent treatment without explanation

- Posting vague social media content aimed at specific people
- Bringing other friends into the drama to pick sides

Responding looks like:

- Figuring out what you're really upset about
- Addressing the person directly instead of through other people
- Using "I" statements to express how you feel
- Focusing on solving the problem instead of winning the fight
- Considering the other person's perspective before jumping to conclusions

When we're stressed from school pressure like test anxiety or grade worries, our emotional reactions get bigger and faster. The skills you've been building throughout this book become even more important when friendship drama hits.

The 24-Hour Rule

For big conflicts, write an angry message but don't send it. Get all your feelings out on paper or in a draft text. Let yourself feel mad, hurt, or disappointed. Then sleep on it.

Tomorrow, read what you wrote and ask yourself:

- Will sending this help or hurt the situation?

- What am I really trying to accomplish here?
- Is there a way to express this that doesn't attack the other person?
- What would I want someone to say to me if roles were reversed?

Most of the time, you'll find a much better way to handle things after you've cooled down.

Assertive Scripts That Actually Work

Instead of letting emotions drive your words, try these approaches:

Instead of: "Wow, nice to know where I stand."

Try: "I felt left out when I saw those posts. Can we talk about what's going on between us?"

Instead of: "You never have time for me anymore."

Try: "I miss spending time together. Can we figure out a way to hang out more?"

Instead of: "I can't believe you said that about me."

Try: "When you said that, it really hurt my feelings. I don't think you meant it that way, but can we talk about it?"

Notice how these scripts focus on your feelings rather than attacking the other person's character. They also open the door for conversation instead of shutting it down.

The Real Issue Check

Before you dive into any friendship conflict, ask yourself: "Am I mad about this specific thing, or is this about something bigger?"

Often we fight about surface-level stuff when we're really upset about deeper issues:

- Feeling replaced or left out
- Sensing that someone is pulling away
- Worrying that you're not as important to them as they are to you
- Feeling like your friend doesn't understand or support you anymore

Isaiah was furious when his friend group made weekend plans without him. His first instinct was to post something petty on social media. Instead, he used the pause technique we learned earlier and realized he'd been declining their invites for weeks because of work stress. He reached out directly: "Hey, I saw you guys hung out. I know I've been flaky lately because of my job, but I miss hanging with everyone. Can we figure out something that works?" The conversation revealed they thought he wasn't interested anymore, and they easily worked it out.

Sometimes the real issue isn't what your friend did—it's about your own insecurities or assumptions.

Setting Up Success

These friendship skills you're building will be crucial as we move into our next chapter about social anxiety. Learning to navigate conflicts calmly gives you confidence in all your social interactions, even when you're feeling nervous about showing up in group settings.

Truth Bombs and Screenshot Wars

Someone screenshot your private message and now it's making the rounds with added commentary you never said. Your mentions are blowing up with people you barely know having opinions about your business. The urge to defend yourself, post receipts, and drag everyone involved feels overwhelming. But here's the thing about digital drama—participating usually makes it worse, not better.

Remember those traffic light emotions we talked about earlier? Online conflicts can send you straight to red-light territory faster than almost anything else. The anger and hurt you feel when someone twists your words or shares your private business can be intense and immediate.

Why Digital Drama Hits Different

Online conflicts spread faster and hit harder than face-to-face drama because there's no tone of voice, no body language, and no easy way to have a real conversation. Plus, there's an audience watching, which makes everything feel more high-stakes and public.

Think about it—when you're mad at someone in person, you can see their facial expressions, hear their actual tone, and gauge whether they're genuinely trying to hurt you or if something got lost in translation. Online, a simple "okay" can feel dismissive and rude when it might just mean they're busy.

The screenshot culture makes everything worse. People save messages, crop them to remove context, and share them with commentary that changes the whole meaning. Suddenly, your private conversation becomes public entertainment.

The Golden Rule of Digital Drama

Don't feed the beast. Drama needs engagement to survive. Screenshots, quote tweets, response videos, and calling people out in your stories are all feeding it. When you starve drama of attention, it usually dies much faster.

This doesn't mean you have to take abuse or let people spread lies about you. It means being smart about how and when you respond.

Instead of public responses, try:

- Taking screenshots for your own records, then ignoring it
- Reaching out privately to address the real issue
- Asking trusted friends not to share drama screenshots with you
- Focusing your energy on people and activities that actually matter
- Using the 24-hour rule before responding to anything inflammatory

The Private Message Rule

If someone has an issue with you online, respond privately with something like: "I'd rather talk about this in person or over the phone." This takes the drama out of the public eye and gives you both a chance to actually communicate instead of performing for an audience.

Most people who start drama online don't actually want to resolve anything—they want attention and validation. When you refuse to give them a public platform, they often lose interest quickly.

Digital Evidence Protection

Before posting anything, ask yourself: "How would this look if someone screenshot it and shared it out of context?" This applies to:

- Private messages that could be shared
- Stories or posts about specific people
- Comments about other people's drama
- Anything you write when you're angry or upset
- Photos and videos that could be misinterpreted

Once you post something, you lose control over how it gets used. Even if you delete it later, someone might have already saved it.

When Drama Finds You Anyway

Daisy found out that someone had been spreading rumors about her in a group chat she wasn't in. Friends were sending her screenshots and asking if she wanted to "expose" the person. Instead of joining the drama, she messaged the rumor-starter directly: "I heard there's been some confusion about me. I'd rather clear this up between us than have it play out online."

It turned out to be a misunderstanding that they resolved in one conversation. Meanwhile, the people trying to "help" by sharing screenshots had actually made the rumors spread further.

Sometimes the best move is addressing things head-on, but privately. Sometimes it's ignoring the situation completely. The key is thinking strategically instead of just reacting emotionally.

Building Your Digital Confidence

The skills you're learning about managing anger and responding rather than reacting apply just as much online as they do in person. Actually, they might be even more important online where everything moves faster and feels more intense.

As we move into the next chapter about social anxiety, remember that a lot of social nervousness comes from worrying about being judged or misunderstood. Learning to handle digital drama confidently builds your overall social confidence too.

Words Left Unspoken

You're lying in bed at 2am replaying that argument from three weeks ago, thinking of all the perfect comebacks you should have said. Or worse, you're cringing at what you actually said when you were angry. The "cringe spiral" is real, and it can keep you stuck in shame instead of learning from what happened.

This late-night mental replay happens to everyone. Your brain is trying to process and make sense of what went wrong, but without a plan for it just becomes torture.

Everyone has moments they wish they could take back. The goal isn't to be perfect—it's to get better at recognizing patterns, making amends when needed, and having a plan for next time.

The Do-Over Exercise

Instead of just replaying your mistakes, try this: Write out what you wish you had said or done differently. This isn't about dwelling on the past—it's about training your brain for better responses in the future.

Start with the situation that keeps bugging you. Then ask:

- What was I really feeling underneath the anger?
- What did I actually want to communicate?
- How could I have expressed that without attacking the other person?
- What would have been a better way to handle my emotions in that moment?

Write out a script of how you wish the conversation had gone. This gives your brain a blueprint for similar situations in the future. It also helps you separate what you were really trying to say from the messy way it came out when you were upset.

The Apology Formula

Sometimes you need to circle back and clean up a mess you made. Here's a simple formula that actually works:

"I'm sorry I [specific action]. I understand that it [impact on them]. Next time I will [specific change]."

Notice what's missing from this apology: excuses, blame-shifting, and "but you did this too" statements.

Example: "I'm sorry I yelled at you about the dishes when you were trying to tell me about your day. I understand it made you feel like I don't care about what's important to you. Next time I'm feeling overwhelmed, I'll ask for a few minutes to decompress before we talk."

This formula works because it takes responsibility, shows you understand the impact, and gives the other person confidence that things will be different next time.

Pattern Recognition

Look for themes in your regrets. Do you always snap when you're hungry? Get defensive when you feel criticized? Start arguments when you're stressed about school like we talked about in the previous chapter?

Common anger patterns include:

- Hangry explosions - anger that's really about being tired or hungry
- Stress overflow - taking out school or work frustration on family

- Criticism sensitivity - getting defensive when you feel judged
- Control reactions - getting angry when you feel powerless
- Overwhelm snapping - lashing out when too many demands hit at once

Once you know your patterns, you can prepare for them. If you always get cranky when you're hungry, keep snacks around. If you explode after stressful days at school, build in decompression time before family interactions.

Learning from Real Mistakes

Marcus had a huge fight with his dad where he said some really hurtful things about his parents' divorce. He felt terrible but was too embarrassed to bring it up again. Using the do-over exercise, he wrote out what he really meant: that he was scared about the changes happening, not actually angry at his dad for trying to make the best of it.

A week later, he used that script to have an actual conversation with his dad, which led to them being closer than they'd been in months. His dad even thanked him for coming back to clean up the mess instead of just hoping it would blow over.

The vulnerability of admitting you messed up often strengthens relationships rather than weakening them.

Chapter Recap

Anger is usually a messenger for other emotions—hurt, fear, or feeling powerless. The key to managing it isn't to never get angry, but to catch it early and respond instead of react.

At home, this means recognizing your yellow-light warning signs and asking for what you need before you hit red. In friendships, it means pausing before you send that text and getting curious about what's really bothering you. Online, it means refusing to feed the drama beast and taking conflicts private.

And when you do mess up, because everyone does, it means owning it, learning from it, and doing better next time.

Your Action Steps

Start using the traffic light system this week—notice when you're at yellow and what your body is telling you. Practice the 24-hour rule for your next frustrating text conversation. Create a "do-over" entry in your notes app for a recent conflict you wish had gone differently.

Most importantly, remember that learning to manage anger is a skill that takes practice, not a personality flaw you need to fix.

While this chapter focused on managing anger and conflict with people you're already close to, the next chapter tackles a different kind of emotional challenge—the anxiety that comes with social situations where you're not sure where you stand or how you'll be received.

Let's explore how to show up authentically even when your brain is telling you to hide.

Chapter 6: Social Anxiety

Showing Up When You Want to Hide

When All Eyes Turn Your Way

Picture this: You're walking into the cafeteria and suddenly feel like everyone's eyes are glued to you. Your backpack feels heavier, your walk feels awkward, and you're convinced the entire school is judging your outfit choice. Sound familiar? Welcome to the spotlight effect—the feeling that you're constantly being watched and evaluated, even when you're just existing.

Here's the reality check: Most people are way too busy worrying about themselves to scrutinize your every move. The spotlight effect tricks your brain into thinking you're the main character in everyone else's story, when actually, you're barely a background character in most people's daily thoughts. Understanding this can be your first step toward freedom.

The Evidence Against the Spotlight:

- The 90-Second Rule: Most people's attention spans are incredibly short. Even if someone does notice something about you, they'll likely forget it within 90 seconds because something else grabs their attention.
- The Phone Test: Look around any public space and count how many people are looking at their phones versus looking at other people. You'll quickly realize that most people are absorbed in their own digital worlds.
- The Memory Challenge: Try to remember what three random classmates wore yesterday. Can't do it? Neither can they about you.

Abigail used to spend twenty minutes every morning choosing her outfit, convinced that everyone would judge her if she wore the wrong thing. She'd change three times and still feel anxious walking into school. After learning about the spotlight effect, she started timing herself getting ready and challenging her thoughts. When she caught herself thinking "Everyone will think this looks stupid," she'd counter with "Most people won't even notice, and if they do, they'll forget in two minutes." Within a month, her morning routine went from stressful to manageable, and she realized that her confidence came from how she felt about herself, not from avoiding imaginary judgment.

But knowing about the spotlight effect is just the beginning. Social anxiety runs deeper than worrying about being watched. It's that stomach-churning feeling when you have to speak up in class, the racing heart when someone calls your name unexpectedly, or the overwhelming urge to disappear when you walk into a room full of people.

Remember how we talked about cooling down anger in the last chapter? Social anxiety works similarly to anger because it triggers your fight-or-flight response, but instead of wanting to fight, your brain screams, "RUN AWAY!" The same breathing techniques that help with anger can absolutely help with social anxiety.

Quick Anxiety Reset Techniques:

- The 4-7-8 Breath: Breathe in for 4 counts, hold for 7, exhale for 8. This activates your calm-down system.
- The 5-4-3-2-1 Grounding Method: Notice 5 things you can see, 4 things you can touch, 3 things you can hear, 2 things you can smell, and 1 thing you can taste.
- The Confidence Pose: Stand tall with your shoulders back for 30 seconds. Your body language actually influences how confident you feel.

Social anxiety often makes us think in extremes. We imagine the worst potential outcome and treat it like it's guaranteed to happen. But most social situations fall somewhere in the middle—not amazing, not terrible, just normal human interactions.

Think about it this way: When someone else trips in the hallway, do you laugh and remember it forever, or do you maybe glance over and then immediately go back to your own thoughts? Most people are surprisingly kind and forgiving, especially when they remember times they've been in similar situations.

Social anxiety also feeds on avoidance. The more you skip social situations, the scarier they become in your mind. It's like avoiding a math test—the longer you put it off, the more terrifying it seems, even though the actual test might be easier than you imagined.

This connects perfectly to what we'll explore in the next chapter about communication skills. Learning to speak your truth becomes much easier when you're not paralyzed by the fear of judgment.

The goal isn't to eliminate social anxiety completely—some nervousness in social situations is totally normal and even helpful. The goal is to show up anyway, knowing that you can handle whatever happens, and that most people are rooting for you to succeed rather than hoping you'll fail.

From Wallflower to Team Player

Group projects can feel like social anxiety's final boss battle. You're dealing with forced interaction, performance pressure, and the fear of looking stupid all rolled into one assignment. Add in the complexity of different personalities, work styles, and the dreaded moment when the teacher says "pick your own groups," and it's enough to make anyone want to fake sick.

The key to surviving group work isn't becoming a different person—it's working with your natural tendencies while building small confidence muscles. Social anxiety often comes with the superpower of being a brilliant listener and observer, which are actually valuable group skills that many people lack.

Strategic Approaches for Group Success:

- The Preparation Safety Net: Before any group meeting, write 2-3 ideas or questions on a small piece of paper. Having this "cheat sheet" gives you something to contribute even if your mind goes blank.
- The Soft Entry Strategy: Use phrases like "Building on what Frank said..." or "I might be wrong, but what if..." to ease into conversations without feeling like you need to make a grand statement.
- The Role Strategy: Volunteer for behind-the-scenes roles that play to your strengths—research, organization, or editing—rather than forcing yourself into the presenter role if that feels overwhelming.

Frank dreaded group projects because he felt like he never had good ideas and worried about speaking up. His strategy became arriving early to meetings with a few conversation starters written, like "What if we focused on..." or "I found this interesting point about..." He also started volunteering to be the note-taker, which gave him a legitimate reason to listen more than talk while still contributing meaningfully. By the end of the semester, his group members were specifically asking to work with him because he kept everyone organized and always came prepared. He realized that being the "quiet, thoughtful one" was actually a strength, not a weakness.

Remember those anger management techniques from Chapter 5? They work wonders for group anxiety too. When you feel that familiar panic rising during a heated group discussion, use the same breathing techniques that help cool down anger. The 4-7-8 breathing pattern can reset your nervous system in under a minute, giving you back access to your thinking brain.

Building Social Confidence Step by Step:

The beauty of group projects is that they provide low-stakes practice for real-world collaboration. Each small success builds your confidence bank, proving to your anxious brain that you can handle social challenges.

Start with micro-goals instead of trying to become the group leader overnight. Maybe your goal for the first meeting is simply to ask one clarifying question. For the second meeting, perhaps you share one research finding. These tiny wins accumulate to build genuine confidence.

- The Question Strategy: Asking good questions makes you look engaged and thoughtful. Try "What do you think about..." or "How should we handle..." to show you're thinking critically.

- The Agreement Plus: When you agree with someone, add a minor detail. "Yes, and we could also consider..." This shows you're listening while contributing your own thoughts.

- The Timeline Helper: Offer to keep track of deadlines or create a shared document. Being organized is a valuable role that doesn't require being the loudest voice.

Social anxiety often makes us think that everyone else is naturally confident and socially skilled. But here's a secret: most people feel awkward in group situations sometimes. The difference is that some people have learned to act despite the awkwardness, while others let the fear stop them from participating.

Think about the spotlight effect we discussed earlier. When you're worried about saying something wrong in your group, remember that everyone else is probably more focused on their own performance than judging yours. That embarrassing moment you're replaying in your head? Your group members have likely forgotten it already because they're busy worrying about their own contributions.

Group work also prepares you perfectly for the communication skills we'll dive into in the next chapter. Learning to speak your truth becomes much easier when you've practiced expressing ideas in smaller, structured settings like study groups or project teams.

The goal isn't to become the most talkative person in the group—it's to find your authentic way of contributing. Some people lead with big ideas, others excel at careful planning, and still others shine at bringing out the best in their teammates.

Your social anxiety might always whisper warnings about group situations, but you don't have to let it decide. You can acknowledge the fear, use your coping strategies, and show up anyway.

When Your Finger Hovers Over Delete

That moment when your chest tightens, your palms get sweaty, and every cell in your body screams "GET OUT OF HERE NOW"—that's your fight-or-flight response in action. When social situations feel overwhelming, your brain treats them like physical threats and floods your system with stress hormones designed to help you escape danger. The problem? A group presentation isn't actually a tiger attack, even though your body can't tell the difference.

The urge to ghost—whether it's skipping class, leaving a party early, or avoiding plans altogether—often feels like the only way to get relief. But here's the thing: every time you give in to that urge, you accidentally teach your brain that the situation really was dangerous, making it even harder next time.

Strategic Exit Planning:

- The 10-Minute Rule: Before leaving any situation, commit to staying for 10 more minutes. Often, the initial panic wave will pass, and you'll find you can handle more than you thought.

- The Cost-Benefit Check: Ask yourself, "Will I regret missing this more than I'll regret the discomfort of staying?" Sometimes the answer is genuinely that you should leave, and that's okay too.

- The Mini-Exit Strategy: Instead of leaving entirely, take a bathroom break, step outside for air, or find a quieter corner. Sometimes you just need a reset, not a full retreat.

Faith had a pattern of making plans with friends and then canceling last minute because her anxiety would spike right before leaving the house. She felt terrible about constantly flaking but didn't know how to push through the panic. She started using the 10-minute rule: she'd set a timer and tell herself she only had to stay for 10 minutes, then she could leave guilt-free. Most of the time, after 10 minutes, the worst of her anxiety had passed, and she'd end up staying longer. On days when she still felt overwhelmed after 10 minutes, she'd use a mini-exit—going to the bathroom to do breathing exercises or stepping outside to text her mom. This approach helped her stop the all-or-nothing thinking that was keeping her isolated.

The physical symptoms of social anxiety can feel intense and scary, but remember what we learned about emotions in Chapter 1—they're temporary visitors, not permanent residents. That racing heart and shaky voice don't mean you're doing something wrong; they mean your nervous system is trying to protect you, even when protection isn't needed.

Working With Your Body Instead of Against It:

When you feel that familiar surge of anxiety, don't force it away immediately. Instead, acknowledge what's happening: "My heart is racing because my brain thinks this situation is dangerous, but I'm actually safe." This simple recognition can help short-circuit the panic spiral.

Use the same breathing techniques that work for cooling down anger from Chapter 5. The 4-7-8 breath pattern works especially well for social anxiety because it gives your hands something to do while activating your body's calm down response. Count on your fingers if it helps—most people will assume you're checking the time.

Building Your Tolerance Gradually:

Think of social situations like exercise. You wouldn't expect to run a marathon without training, and you shouldn't expect to handle high-stress social events without building up your tolerance first. Start with lower-pressure situations and work your way up.

- Low-pressure practice: Asking a cashier how their day is going
- Medium-pressure practice: Contributing one comment during a class discussion
- Higher-pressure practice: Attending a party where you only know the host

The goal isn't to eliminate anxiety completely—some nervousness before social events is totally normal. The goal is to show up despite the discomfort and prove to yourself that you can handle whatever happens.

Remember the spotlight effect we discussed earlier? When you're convinced everyone is watching you struggle with anxiety, remind yourself that most people are focused on their own experience. That person who seems so confident? They might deal with their own internal worries that you can't see.

Social anxiety often comes with a harsh inner critic that says things like, "You're being ridiculous" or "Everyone else can handle this." But you wouldn't criticize a friend for having anxiety, so why treat yourself that way? Practice the same self-compassion you'd offer someone else.

This tolerance-building approach sets you up perfectly for the communication skills we'll explore in the next chapter. Learning to speak your truth becomes much easier when you're not fighting a full-scale panic response every time you open your mouth.

The courage to stay isn't about being fearless—it's about being afraid and showing up, anyway.

Hallway Meltdown and Finding Center

School hallways can be emotional minefields. Between classes, you might run into your ex-best friend who's been spreading rumors, the group that didn't invite you to their party, or that person who made a comment about your presentation last week. When you're already feeling vulnerable, these unexpected encounters can send your anxiety through the roof—and you can't exactly have a meltdown in front of your locker.

Public grounding is about having a toolkit of techniques that are invisible to others but powerful for you. These are strategies that help you stay present and calm without anyone knowing you're using them, giving you the confidence to handle whatever the hallway throws your way.

Invisible Anxiety Management:

- The 5-4-3-2-1 Technique: Silently identify 5 things you can see, 4 things you can touch, 3 things you can hear, 2 things you can smell, and 1 thing you can taste. This grounds you in the present moment instead of spiraling into anxious thoughts.

- The Mantra Method: Develop a few short phrases you can repeat silently: "I am safe, this will pass," "Keep walking, keep breathing," or "Their opinion doesn't define me." Having these ready prevents your mind from creating disaster stories.

- The Anchor Touch: Choose something you always carry—a ring, bracelet, or even just pressing your thumb to your palm—as a physical anchor that reminds you that you're okay and this feeling is temporary.

Tyler used to get panic attacks whenever he saw his former friend group in the hallway after their falling out. His heart would race, his face would get hot, and he'd feel like everyone was staring at the drama. He started practicing the 5-4-3-2-1 technique during these encounters: counting ceiling tiles, feeling his backpack straps, listening for specific sounds like locker doors or footsteps. He also developed a simple mantra: "Keep walking, keep breathing, almost there." Having these tools made him realize he could handle the discomfort without it ruining his whole day. Eventually, seeing them became just another part of navigating the hallway rather than a crisis that derailed his mood.

Remember the breathing techniques we discussed for anger management in Chapter 5? They work just as well for social anxiety. The 4-7-8 breath can be done while walking to class, sitting at your desk, or even while talking to someone. Nobody needs to know you're using it.

Creating Your Safety Plan:

The key to managing social anxiety is having a plan before you need it. When you're in the middle of a panic response, your thinking brain goes offline, so you need these techniques to be automatic.

Practice your grounding techniques when you're calm so they're ready when you need them. Try the 5-4-3-2-1 method while sitting in a peaceful place at home, or practice your mantras while walking your dog. The more familiar these tools become, the more naturally they'll come to you during stressful moments.

Also remember the spotlight effect—that feeling that everyone is watching you have an anxious moment? Most people are so caught up in their own drama and worries that they're not analyzing your facial expressions or body language. That person walking past you is probably thinking about their next class, not judging whether you look nervous.

Building Confidence Through Small Wins:

Each time you successfully use these techniques, you're proving to your brain that you can handle difficult social situations. This builds what psychologists call self-efficacy—the belief that you can manage challenges.

Start tracking these minor victories. Did you make it through a crowded cafeteria without leaving early? Did you stay calm when you ran into someone who makes you anxious? These moments matter more than you might think. They're evidence that you're stronger than your anxiety wants you to believe.

The goal isn't to never feel anxious—it's to feel anxious and still be able to function. Some nervousness in social situations is completely normal. The difference between people who seem confident and those who feel paralyzed by anxiety often isn't the absence of nervous feelings—it's knowing how to manage those feelings effectively.

Looking Forward:

Mastering these public grounding techniques sets you up perfectly for what comes next. Once you can stay calm and present in social situations, you're ready to work on expressing yourself authentically. The next chapter will teach you communication skills that help you speak your truth clearly and kindly, even when you're feeling nervous.

Because here's the thing: managing your anxiety is just the first step. The real goal is building genuine connections with people who appreciate the real you. And that requires not just showing up, but speaking up too.

The courage you're building by working through social anxiety will serve you well as we explore how to communicate your needs, set boundaries, and build the relationships you actually want.

Chapter 7: Communication Skills

Speaking Your Truth

When Parents Just Don't Get It

Picture this: You walk into the kitchen after a brutal day at school, and your mom asks how your day was. When you try to explain that you're overwhelmed by three tests next week and your friend group is being weird, she responds with, "" they hear hyperbole. When you say, "I'm stressed about my chemistry test because I missed two days when I was sick and now I'm behind," they hear a problem they can actually help solve.

Think about it from their perspective for a moment. They've been out of high school for decades, and the emotional intensity of teenage life can feel foreign to them now. They remember being your age, but they've forgotten how overwhelming it can feel when your best friend stops texting you back or when you bomb a presentation in front of the entire class.

The Translation Strategy

Your emotions are valid, but sometimes you need to package them differently for adult consumption. Here's how to bridge that communication gap:

- Use the feeling formula: "I feel [specific emotion] because [concrete reason] and I need [specific help or support]." Instead of "I'm freaking out," try "I feel anxious because I have three tests this week and I need help to figure out a study schedule."
- Give them context they can relate to: Compare your situation to something from their world. "You know how stressed you feel when you have multiple deadlines at work? That's how I feel about this week."
- Pick your timing: Don't have deep conversations when they're rushing to work or dealing with their own stress. Ask, "When would be a good time to talk about something that's bothering me?"
- Be specific about what you need: Do you want advice, emotional support, or just someone to listen? Parents often jump straight into problem-solving mode when sometimes you just need validation.

Real Talk Examples

Elizabeth used to get frustrated when her dad would dismiss her friendship drama as "silly girl problems." She started using the formula approach: "I feel hurt because Elizabeth shared something I told her in confidence, and I need advice on whether I should talk to her about it." Her dad's response completely changed—instead of dismissing her feelings, he started sharing stories about his own friendship challenges and offering genuine advice.

Finn struggled with his mom's constant questions about his grades. Instead of getting defensive and shutting down, he learned to say, "I feel pressured when you ask about my grades every day because it makes me think you don't trust me to handle my responsibilities. I need you to trust that I'll come to you if I'm struggling."

When They Still Don't Get It

Sometimes, even with perfect communication, your parents might not understand. This doesn't mean your feelings are wrong or that you should stop trying to communicate. It might mean you need additional support from school counselors, trusted teachers, or other family members who can help bridge the gap.

Remember the emotional regulation techniques we covered in earlier chapters. Your parents' response (or lack of understanding) doesn't have to determine your emotional state. You can acknowledge their limitations while still honoring your own feelings and needs.

Setting the Stage for Harder Conversations

As we move forward, you'll face even tougher emotional challenges—rejection, loss, and major disappointments. The communication skills you're building now with everyday frustrations will serve as your foundation for navigating those more intense situations with your parents and other important adults in your life.

Creating Your Personal Sanctuary at Home

Your bedroom door is closed, you're finally decompressing from a long day, and suddenly there's a knock. "What are you doing in there? Come, hang out with the family!" Your parents mean your need for space isn't too much either. It's actually a healthy coping strategy that helps you process your feelings and reset your energy levels.

Many parents interpret closed doors and requests for an alone time as rejection or signs that something is wrong. They remember when you were little and wanted to tell them everything, so your need for privacy can feel like a loss. The goal is to reassure them that you're okay while still getting the space you need to manage your emotions and energy.

Setting Boundaries That Work

The communication skills we've been building throughout this book become super important when you're trying to create a space at home. Here's how to ask for what you need:

- Reassure first, then request: "I love spending time with you, and I need about an hour to decompress before I can be good company. Can we hang out after dinner instead?"

- Offer a check-in compromise: "I need some alone time right now, but can I come find you in an hour to tell you about my day?" This gives them something to look forward to while respecting your boundary.
- Explain my recharge process: "When I'm overwhelmed, I need quiet time to sort through my thoughts. It actually helps me to be less moody later." Help them understand that space prevents meltdowns rather than causing them.
- Be consistent: If you say you'll emerge in an hour, actually do it. Following through builds trust and makes future requests easier.

Making Your Space Work for You

Your room or designated quiet space should help you practice the emotional regulation techniques we've covered. Think of it as your personal reset zone where you can use the breathing exercises from Chapter 5 when you're angry, or work through social anxiety using the techniques from Chapter 6.

Consider what helps you feel calm and centered. Maybe it's soft lighting, plants, your favorite playlist, or just a clean, organized space. You don't need expensive decorations—even arranging your books in a way that makes you happy can help your space feel more peaceful.

Real-Life Success Stories

Ryan was constantly battling his mom about his need for an alone time after school. She would take it personally when he went straight to his room, thinking he was angry with her. He started using the "reassure and request" approach: "Mom, I had a really draining day and I need thirty minutes to reset. Then I'll come help with dinner and tell you about my history presentation." His mom stopped taking his need for space as rejection and started respecting his routine.

Beth struggled with her dad's habit of barging into her room without knocking. Instead of getting into shouted matches, she had a calm conversation during a suitable moment: "Dad, I really value our relationship, and I need you to knock and wait for me to say 'come in' before entering my room. It helps me feel respected and makes me want to share more with you." Her dad was surprised but agreed, and their relationship actually improved.

When Family Dynamics Are Challenging

Not every family situation is straightforward. If you're dealing with parents who don't respect boundaries despite your best communication efforts, remember that you can still create emotional space even when physical space is limited. This might mean using headphones, going for walks, or finding other family members or adults who can help advocate for your needs.

Your need for space and emotional regulation isn't a luxury—it's essential for your mental health. As we move into the next chapter about handling rejection and loss, having a solid foundation of self-care and personal space will become even more important for weathering life's bigger challenges.

Sharp Words, Softer Landing

Someone makes a snide comment about your outfit, your grades, or your weekend plans. Your blood boils, and you want to either disappear or unleash a savage comeback that will destroy them. But there's a middle ground between being a doormat and being mean—it's called assertiveness, and it's actually more powerful than extreme.

The goal of a sympathetic response isn't to hurt the other person; it's to stand up for yourself while maintaining your dignity. When you respond with class instead of cruelty, you show their words don't have the power to make you lose control. Plus, you avoid the regret that comes with saying something truly harsh in the heat of the moment.

Remember the emotional regulation techniques we covered in Chapter 5 about anger management? Those breathing exercises and pause strategies become super useful when someone is trying to push your buttons. Taking that moment to breathe gives you space to choose your response instead of just reacting.

Your Assertiveness Toolkit

These responses work because they acknowledge what happened without giving the other person the dramatic reaction they might be looking for:

- Use the calm redirect: "That's an interesting opinion" or "I'll take that into consideration" said with a neutral tone shows you heard them but aren't accepting their judgment as fact.
- Set a boundary with humor: "Wow, that was rude," says

with a slight smile, calls out their behavior without escalating the situation. Sometimes, acknowledging the awkwardness is enough to shut it down.

- The confident clarification: "Actually, I'm thrilled with my choice" or "That works for me" shows that their disapproval doesn't affect your decisions. You're not arguing—you're just stating your position.
- The information diet: "I'm not looking for feedback on that" or "That wasn't really a question" lets them know you're not interested in their unsolicited opinions.
- The graceful exit: "I'm going to step away from this conversation" gives you permission to remove yourself from toxic situations without explanation.

Reading the Situation

Not every mean comment deserves a response. Sometimes the most powerful thing you can do is absolutely nothing. If someone is clearly trying to get a rise out of you, ignoring them completely can be more effective than engaging. But when you choose to respond, make it count.

Think about your relationship with this person, and what you're trying to accomplish. Is this someone you need to maintain a relationship with, like a classmate you'll see every day? Or is this a random person whose opinion genuinely doesn't matter? Your response strategy might be different for each situation.

Real-World Examples

Keira used to either ignore mean comments completely (which made her feel weak) or fire back with equally cruel responses (which made her feel guilty later). When Keira made a sarcastic comment about her "trying too hard" with her outfit, instead of staying silent or insulting Keira's style, she says, "I like putting effort into how I look—it makes me feel good." Keira didn't have a comeback for that kind of confidence, and Keira felt proud of how she handled it.

Michael struggled with classmates making jokes about his good grades. Instead of either hiding his intelligence or getting defensive, he started responding with, "Yeah, I work hard and it pays off." His calm confidence actually made some of the teasing stop because he wasn't giving them the embarrassed reaction they expected.

Building Your Confidence Foundation

The communication skills we're developing here will become even more important as we move into the next chapter about handling rejection and loss. Learning to respond to everyday rudeness with grace builds your emotional strength for bigger challenges ahead.

When you can handle small slights with confidence and class, you're building the emotional muscles you'll need when life throws harder stuff your way. Each time you choose a thoughtful response over a reactive one, you're proving to yourself that you have control over your emotional responses.

Practice these techniques in low-stakes situations so they become natural when the pressure is higher.

Friends, Limits, and the Art of Refusing

Your friend wants you to skip lunch to help her study for a test she forgot about. Another friend keeps venting to you about the same problem, taking none of your advice. Your group chat is blowing up with plans for the weekend, but you're exhausted and just want to stay home. Saying no to friends feels terrible because you don't want to let them down, but constantly saying yes when you mean no will eventually make you resent them.

Good friends actually want you to be honest about your limits because fake yeses lead to actual problems. When you say yes but feel bitter about it, or when you agree to plans and then bail last minute because you're overwhelmed, it damages the friendship more than an upfront no would have. Setting boundaries isn't about being selfish—it's about being authentic so your friendships can be genuine.

Think about the social anxiety we discussed in Chapter 6. Sometimes we say yes to things because we're afraid of disappointing people or being left out. But people-pleasing actually makes social situations more stressful because you're constantly doing things you don't want to do. Real confidence comes from knowing you can say no and still be valued as a friend.

Saying No With Grace

Here are scripts that maintain your relationships while protecting your energy:

- The clear but kind script: "I can't tonight, I'm really drained and need to recharge" or "I'm not able to help with that, but I hope your studying goes well." You don't need to over-explain or justify your no.

- Offer an alternative when possible: "I can't hang out Friday, but would Saturday afternoon work?" or "I can't help you study, but Gregory is really good at chemistry—maybe ask him?"

- Handle the guilt trip gracefully: If they respond with "You never want to hang out anymore" or "I guess I'll just fail then," stay calm: "I understand you're disappointed. I'm not available tonight, but I care about you and our friendship."

- The broken record technique: Keep repeating your boundary in different words if they keep pushing. "I understand this is important to you, and I'm still not available."

When Friends Cross Lines

Sometimes the issue isn't a single request but a pattern of behavior that makes you uncomfortable. Maybe a friend constantly interrupts you, makes jokes at your expense, or pressures you to do things you're not comfortable with. These situations require the communication skills we've been building throughout this chapter.

Use the feeling formula we discussed earlier: "I feel uncomfortable when you make jokes about my weight because it hurts my feelings, and I need you to stop." Be direct but not mean. Good friends will adjust their behavior when you point out that it's bothering you.

Real-Life Example

Gregory was the friend everyone came to with their problems, and while he enjoyed being helpful, it was draining him. When Gregory called crying about the same relationship drama for the third time that week, instead of listening for another hour while feeling frustrated, he said, "I can see this is really hard for you. I think talking to the school counselor might be more helpful than I am right now—they have better advice for this kind of situation." Gregory was initially hurt, but later thanked him for being honest and ended up getting professional help that actually worked.

Building Stronger Friendship amps Through Boundaries

When you're honest about your limits, you create space for more authentic connections. Your friends get to know the real you, not just the version that always says yes. And when you do say yes to hanging out or helping them, they know you genuinely want to be there.

Remember the emotional regulation techniques from earlier chapters. When you feel guilty about setting a boundary, use the breathing exercises from Chapter 5 to stay calm. Remind yourself that protecting your energy isn't selfish—it's necessary for being a good friend in the long run.

Preparing for Bigger Challenges

Learning to communicate your needs with friends builds confidence for handling harder situations. Sometimes even the best communication skills can't prevent painful experiences like being excluded, losing a friendship, or facing major disappointments. The foundation you're building now—knowing how to express yourself clearly and set healthy boundaries—will serve you well when life throws bigger challenges your way.

Chapter 8: Rejection and Loss

Handling the Hard Stuff

The Sting of Being Invisible

You checked your phone for the fifth time in ten minutes. The group chat that was buzzing yesterday has gone silent—at least for you. You see the subtle signs: plans being made without you, inside jokes you're not part of, that sinking feeling when you realize you're on the outside looking in.

Social rejection hits differently because humans are literally wired for connection. When we're excluded, our brains process it like physical pain. That ache in your chest? It's real, and it's valid.

Remember what we learned about speaking your truth in the last chapter? Sometimes rejection happens because we haven't been clear about our needs or boundaries. Other times, it's completely out of our control. The key is learning to tell the difference and responding with intention rather than desperation.

Understanding the Rejection Response

Your body doesn't know the difference between being chased by a tiger and being left out of a friend group. Both trigger the same alarm system. Your heart pounds, your thoughts race, and you might feel dizzy or sick to your stomach. This is your nervous system doing its job—protecting you from what it perceives as a threat to your survival.

The tricky part is that social rejection often comes with a story. Your brain fills in the gaps: "I'm not good enough," "Everyone hates me," "I'll never fit in anywhere." These thoughts feel true in the moment, but they're usually just your mind trying to make sense of confusing emotions.

The First 48 Hours: Damage Control

In the immediate aftermath of rejection or ghosting is when your most vulnerable to decide you'll regret later. This is when you might send that desperate text, show up uninvited to events, or post passive-aggressive social media content hoping they'll see it and feel bad.

Stop. Breathe. Give yourself space.

Here's your emergency toolkit for the first 48 hours:

- Ground yourself physically: The 5-4-3-2-1 technique helps pull you out of emotional overwhelm. Name 5 things you can see, 4 things you can touch, 3 things you can hear, 2 things you can smell, and 1 thing you can taste.

- Move your body: Rejection floods your system with stress hormones. Physical movement—even just walking around the block—helps your body process and release that energy.

- Limit social media: Set a timer for 15 minutes if you must check, then close the apps. Scrolling through their stories looking for clues about why they're ignoring you only makes the pain worse.

- Call someone safe: Reach out to a friend or family member who consistently shows up for you. You don't have to explain everything—just connect with someone who reminds you that you matter.

Reality-Check Questions

Before you spiral into worst-case scenarios, ask yourself these questions:

- Is this about me, or about them?

- What evidence do I have that this is personal?

- Have they been going through their own stuff lately?

- Is this part of a pattern, or an isolated incident?

Georgia noticed her best friend had been responding to texts with one-word answers and declining invitations to hang out. Instead of assuming she'd done something wrong, Georgia remembered that her friend's parents were going through a divorce. When she gently asked if everything was okay, her friend broke down and admitted she'd been too overwhelmed to maintain normal friendships. The "rejection" had nothing to do with Georgia at all.

When It Really Is About You

Sometimes rejection happens because of something you said or did. This doesn't mean you're a terrible person—it means you're human. We all mess up, say the wrong thing, or hurt people unintentionally.

If you can identify what went wrong, the communication skills from the previous chapter become crucial. A sincere apology acknowledges the impact of your actions without making excuses. "I realize what I said hurt you, and I'm sorry" is more powerful than "I'm sorry you felt hurt by what I said."

Building Rejection Resilience

Each time you survive rejection and come out the other side, you build evidence that you can handle hard things. This doesn't mean the pain gets easier—it means you get stronger.

The most important thing to remember is that rejection is information, not a verdict on your worth as a person. Sometimes it tells you that this isn't your group, this person isn't your person, or this situation isn't right for you.

That's not a failure. That's clarity.

Breaking the "I'm Fine" Lie

There's an unspoken pressure to always be "fine" or "good" when people ask how you're doing. But sometimes you're drowning, and pretending otherwise just makes it worse. Admitting you're struggling isn't weakness—it's self-awareness.

It takes courage to say, "I'm not okay" in a world that rewards putting on a brave face. The fear of being seen as dramatic, attention-seeking, or "too much" keeps many teens suffering in silence. Remember what we learned in Chapter One about your emotions not being "too much"? That applies here too.

The Mask We Wear

You've probably perfected the "I'm fine" mask by now. Smile when you're hurting, laugh when you want to cry, say "everything's good" when your world feels like it's falling apart. This mask becomes so automatic that sometimes you forget you're even wearing it.

The problem with this mask is that it cuts you off from genuine connection and support. When people ask how you're doing, they're offering an opportunity for actual communication—the kind we talked about in the previous chapter. But if you always respond with "fine," you miss the chance to let people see you and help you.

Think about it this way: when a friend says they're struggling, do you think less of them? Do you see them as weak or dramatic? Probably not. You likely feel honored they trusted you enough to be honest. You might even feel closer to them because they shared something real with you.

That's exactly how the right people will respond to your honesty too.

The "Temperature Check" Method

One tool that makes honest communication easier is the emotional temperature check. Rate your emotional state on a scale of 1-10, where 1 means "I'm thriving and feel amazing" and 10 means "I'm in crisis and need immediate help."

This system gives you language for your feelings without requiring a detailed explanation. You can tell someone "I'm at about a 7 today" and they'll understand you're struggling with no need to know all the details right away.

Here's how to use the scale:

- 1-3: You're doing handling challenges with confidence
- 4-6: You're managing okay but feeling some stress or difficult emotions
- 7-8: You're struggling significantly and could really use support
- 9-10: You're in crisis mode and need immediate help from a trusted adult

Anything above a 7 is your signal that it's time to reach out. Don't wait until you hit a 10.

Overcoming Vulnerability Fears

The scariest part about dropping the "I'm fine" mask is the fear of how people will react. What if they judge you? What if they think you're being dramatic? What if they don't know what to say?

Start small. You don't have to share your deepest struggles with everyone. Choose one trusted person—a friend, family member, teacher, or counselor—and practice honest communication with them first.

Isaac had been struggling with depression for months but kept telling everyone he was fine. When his grades started slipping and he stopped hanging out with friends, his older sister noticed. She asks him directly, "On a scale of 1-10, how are you really doing?" Something about the specific question made it easier for him to admit he was at an 8. That conversation led to his getting the support he needed.

Communication Templates

Having a script ready makes it easier to reach out when you're struggling. Your brain doesn't work as clearly when you're overwhelmed, so having these phrases prepared can be a lifesaver:

- "Hey, I'm having a really hard time right now and could use someone to talk to. Are you free?"
- "I'm not doing great today. Can we hang out? I don't need advice, just company."
- "I'm at about an 8 on the stress scale. Could you check in with me later?"

- "I've been struggling lately and could use some support. Do you have time to listen?"

Notice how these templates are specific about what you need. Sometimes you want advice, sometimes just someone to listen, sometimes just company. Being clear about what kind of support you're looking for helps people know how to help you.

Setting the Stage for Resilience

When you practice honest communication about your struggles, you're actually building the foundation for something incredibly important: resilience. Each time you reach out instead of suffering alone, you're proving to yourself that hard times don't have to be faced in isolation.

This skill—asking for help when you need it—is one of the most crucial building blocks of emotional strength. In the next chapter, we'll explore how this vulnerability actually becomes a superpower in bouncing back from life's challenges.

The people who seem the strongest aren't the ones who never fall down. They're the ones who know how to get back up, and they know they don't have to do it alone.

Apologies That Heal

We've all been on the receiving end of a fake apology: "I'm sorry you feel that way" or "Sorry, but you did this too." These non-apologies often make things worse because they don't acknowledge genuine hurt or responsibility. A genuine apology can repair relationships and rebuild trust, but only if it's done right.

Real apologies require you to get uncomfortable, admit fault, and commit to change—which is why they're so powerful.

Think back to the communication skills we covered in the last chapter. Speaking your truth isn't just about expressing your needs—it's also about taking responsibility when you've caused harm. This is where emotional regulation meets relationship repair.

The Anatomy of a Real Apology

Most people think saying "sorry" is enough, but that's just the beginning. A true apology has three essential parts that work together to create genuine healing.

Step 1: Own What You Did Wrong

No excuses, no "but" statements, no shifting blame. You clearly state what you did that caused harm. This isn't about your intentions—it's about your actions and their impact.

Bad example: "I'm sorry I was late, but traffic was crazy."

Good example: "I'm sorry I was late and didn't text you to let you know."

Step 2: Acknowledge the Impact

Show that you understand how your actions affected the other person. This shows empathy and helps them feel heard. You're not just sorry for what you did—you're sorry for how it made them feel.

"I know that made you feel unimportant and like I don't respect your time."

Step 3: Commit to Change

This is where most apologies fall apart. You need to offer specific, concrete steps for how you'll do better. Vague promises like "it won't happen again" don't build trust. Detailed plans do.

"From now on, I'll leave fifteen minutes earlier than I think I need to, and I'll text you if I'm running over five minutes late."

What Kills an Apology

Certain phrases and attitudes can destroy even the most well-intentioned apology. Avoid these common mistakes:

- "But" statements: "I'm sorry I yelled, but you weren't listening." This cancels out everything that came before.
- Blame-shifting: "I'm sorry you misunderstood what I meant." You're not actually taking responsibility here.
- Making it about you: "I feel terrible about this" or "This is so hard for me." The focus should be on the person you hurt.
- Demanding immediate forgiveness: "I said sorry, so we're good now, right?" Healing takes time.
- Minimizing the hurt: "It's not that big of a deal" or "You're

being too sensitive." Let them define their own experience.

Customizing Your Apology

Unique relationships require slightly different approaches, though the three-step structure remains the same.

For Friends:

"I messed up when I [specific action]. I know it hurt you, and I take full responsibility. Here's how I plan to do better..."

For Family:

"I was disrespectful when I [behavior]. I understand why you're upset, and I want to rebuild your trust by..."

For Romantic Relationships:

"I hurt you when I [action], and I can see how that made you feel [emotion]. I'm committed to [specific change]."

Grace had to apologize to her best friend after she canceled their plans last minute for the third time. Instead of making excuses about being busy, she says: "I was wrong to keep canceling on you with little notice. I know it makes you feel you're not a priority, and that's not true. From now on, I'm going to check my schedule before making plans and give you at least twenty-four hours' notice if something comes up." Her friend appreciated the specific commitment to change.

When Apologies Aren't Enough

Sometimes, even perfect apologies can't fix what's broken. The other person might need time to process, or the damage might be too severe for a quick repair. That's okay, and it's not a failure on your part.

Your job is to offer a genuine apology and follow through on your commitments to change. You can't control whether someone accepts your apology, but you can control whether it's worth accepting.

Building Strength Through Accountability

Learning to apologize well is actually a form of emotional strength training. Each time you take genuine responsibility for your mistakes, you're building the kind of character that bounces back from setbacks stronger than before.

This skill—owning your mistakes and making them right—is one of the core building blocks of resilience. People who can apologize authentically are the ones who maintain strong relationships through tough times, and strong relationships are crucial for weathering life's storms.

In our next chapter, we'll explore how this foundation of accountability and honest communication becomes the springboard for developing true resilience.

When Friends Become Strangers

Friendship breakups can hurt just as much as romantic ones, but they get way less recognition. There's no socially acceptable grieving period for when your best friend becomes a stranger, or when a friend group implodes. You're expected to just "get over it" and "make new friends."

But losing a close friendship means losing shared memories, inside jokes, daily texts, and someone who really knew you. That loss deserves to be acknowledged and processed, not minimized.

The Unique Pain of Friendship Loss

Unlike romantic breakups, friendship endings often happen slowly and without clear resolution. One day you realize you haven't talked in weeks, or you notice they're making plans without you, or you simply grow into different people who no longer connect.

Sometimes friendship loss is dramatic—a fight, a betrayal, choosing sides in group drama. Other times it's gradual—interests change, schedules don't align, new priorities take over. Both types of endings can leave you feeling confused and hurt.

The hardest part is that friendship breakups rarely come with closure. There's usually no conversation where you officially end things, no returning belongings, no obvious moment when it's "over." You're left wondering what happened and whether you should try to fix it.

Allowing the Grief Process

Give yourself permission to feel sad, angry, confused, or relieved—sometimes all at once. Friendship grief comes in waves, just like any other loss. Some days you'll miss them intensely; other days you'll feel free.

Both are normal parts of healing.

Your emotions might include:

- Sadness about losing someone who understood you
- Anger if you feel betrayed or abandoned
- Relief if the friendship had become toxic or draining
- Confusion about what went wrong or how to move forward
- Regret about things you said or didn't say
- Fear that you'll never find another friend like them

Remember what we learned back in Chapter One about your emotions not being "too much." This applies to friendship grief too. You're not being dramatic for mourning a meaningful relationship.

Reflection Without Rumination

It's natural to want to understand what happened, but there's a difference between healthy reflection and obsessive rumination. Set aside specific time to think through the friendship—maybe fifteen minutes a day—then redirect your attention when your mind starts spiraling.

Ask yourself growth-oriented questions:

- What did this friendship teach me about myself?
- What kind of friend do I want to be from now on?
- What red flags will I watch for in future friendships?
- What qualities do I value most in close relationships?

- How can I apply the communication skills from Chapter Seven to future friendships?

These questions help you learn from the experience rather than just reliving the pain.

Closure Rituals

Since friendship endings rarely come with natural closure, you might need to create your own. These rituals help your brain process the ending and make space for new connections.

Some meaningful closure activities include:

- Writing a letter you'll never send, expressing everything you wish you could say
- Creating a playlist of songs that remind you of good times together
- Gathering photos and mementos in a box or scrapbook
- Doing something symbolic like deleting old text threads or unfollowing on social media
- Having a conversation with a trusted adult about what the friendship meant to you

Cole and his best friend since elementary school grew apart when they started high school. Different interests, new friend groups, and changing personalities meant they barely talked anymore. Instead of pretending it didn't hurt, he wrote his former friend a letter thanking him for all the wonderful memories and wishing him and that doesn't diminish what it meant to you.

Strength Through Vulnerability and Loss

People change, especially during the teen years. The person who was perfect for you at twelve might not fit your life at sixteen. That's not a failure—it's growth.

Learning to grieve a friendship loss with grace prepares you for one of life's most important skills: resilience. Each time you navigate the end of a meaningful relationship and come out okay on the other side, you build evidence that you can handle hard things.

This experience of loss, as painful as it is, becomes part of your emotional strength training. In the next chapter, we'll explore how these tough experiences—the rejections, the losses, the moments when you had to be vulnerable—all contribute to building the resilience that helps you bounce back from setbacks stronger than before.

Because that's what resilience really is: proof that you can survive hard things and keep growing.

Chapter 9: Resilience Bouncing Back Stronger

When Shame Becomes Your Teacher

Remember how we talked about handling rejection and loss in the last chapter? Those painful experiences taught you something crucial to your inner strength. Now we're going to explore how embarrassing moments, while uncomfortable, can actually become powerful teachers that build your resilience muscle.

We've all been there—that moment when you trip in the hallway, accidentally send a text to the wrong person, or say something that makes everyone go quiet. Your face burns, your stomach drops, and all you want to do is disappear forever. But here's the truth: everyone has cringe moments, and the way you handle them says more about your character than the mistake itself.

Embarrassment feels massive in the moment, but it's actually your brain's way of helping you learn social boundaries. The key isn't avoiding embarrassing moments (impossible) but developing a bounce-back process that helps you recover quickly and maintain your confidence.

The Three-Step Recovery Method:

- The 24-Hour Rule: Most people forget your embarrassing moment within a day, but you might replay it for weeks. Remind yourself that others are too busy worrying about their own lives to focus on your slip-ups.
- The Reframe Technique: Instead of "Everyone thinks I'm stupid," try "I'm human and humans make mistakes." This shifts you from a shame spiral to self-compassion.
- The Story Flip: Ask yourself, "Will this matter in five years?" Usually, the answer is no. Some of your most embarrassing moments might even become funny stories later.

Dorothy was giving a presentation in English class when she completely blanked on her next point and stood there for what felt like forever. Her face turned red, and she wanted to run out of the room. Instead, she took a breath and says, "Let me check my notes real quick." After class, she felt mortified, but her friend tells her, "Honestly, I didn't even notice—I was too worried about my presentation next week." Dorothy realized that her "disaster" barely registered with anyone else, and she used this experience to remind herself that most people are focused on their own concerns, not judging her every move.

The Spotlight Effect

Your brain tricks you into thinking everyone is watching and judging your every move. This is called the spotlight effect, and it's completely normal but rarely accurate. Think about the last time you witnessed someone else's embarrassing moment. How long did you think about it? Probably not very long.

When you mess up, your internal alarm system goes off because your brain wants to keep you safe from social rejection. But in today's world, most embarrassing moments won't actually threaten your safety or relationships. Learning to recognize this can help you calm down faster.

Building Embarrassment Resilience

Start small by practicing self-compassion during minor awkward moments. When you stumble over words or drop something, notice your first reaction. Are you being harsh with yourself or understanding? The same emotional regulation techniques we've discussed throughout this book—like the breathing exercises from Chapter 5 and the reframing strategies from Chapter 2—work perfectly for embarrassing situations too.

Julian used to replay every social mistake for days, analyzing what he should have said differently. After learning about the spotlight effect, he started setting a timer for five minutes whenever he felt embarrassed. He would allow himself to feel the discomfort for those five minutes, then deliberately redirect his attention to something else. This practice helped him realize that dwelling on embarrassment was a choice, not a requirement.

The Growth Mindset Connection

Each embarrassing moment is actually data about how to navigate the world better. Maybe you learned to double-check who you're texting before hitting send. Maybe you discovered that asking for help when you're stuck isn't the end of the world. These lessons build your confidence over time.

The goal isn't to become embarrassment-proof—it's to become embarrassment-resilient.

As we move forward to explore living your truth and building your identity in the next chapter, remember that your ability to recover from awkward moments is actually a superpower. It shows you can handle uncertainty, adapt to unexpected situations, and maintain your sense of self even when things don't go according to plan.

When Stumbles Become Stepping Stones

Remember how we explored handling rejection and loss in the previous chapter? Those painful experiences weren't just obstacles to overcome—they were actually building something powerful inside you. Now we're going to discover how every setback, failure, and disappointment can become raw material for your strongest comeback yet.

Failure isn't the opposite of success—it's a stepping stone to it. Every successful person has a collection of failures behind them, but they learned to see setbacks as data rather than disasters. When you fail a test, get rejected, or mess up a friendship, you're not broken—you're gathering information about what doesn't work so you can try something different next time.

The difference between people who bounce back and those who stay stuck isn't that some never fail—it's that resilient people have learned to mine their failures for useful information. They ask, "What can I learn?" instead of "Why does this always happen to me?"

The Failure-to-Success Framework

Think of failures as rough diamonds. They look ugly and worthless at first, but with the right processing, they become valuable. Here's how to extract the gems from your setbacks:

- The Data Collection Mindset: Treat failures like experiments. What variables can you change next time? What worked, what didn't, and what would you do differently?
- The Comeback Plan: After a setback, create a specific plan for your next attempt. This gives you something to focus on besides the disappointment and puts you back in control.
- Success Story Research: Look up famous people in areas

you care about and learn about their failures. Most successful people failed multiple times before breaking through.

David auditioned for the school play three times and got rejected each time. After the third rejection, he was ready to give up acting completely. But instead of quitting, he asked the drama teacher for specific feedback. She told him his acting was good, but his projection needed work. David spent the summer taking voice lessons and practicing projection exercises. When auditions came around senior year, he not only made the play but landed a lead role. His earlier rejections weren't signs he should quit—they were information about what skills he needed to develop.

Breaking the Failure Shame Spiral

When you fail at something important, your brain might start that familiar loop of self-criticism we discussed back in Chapter 2. But remember those emotional regulation techniques we've been building throughout this book? They work perfectly here too.

First, use the breathing exercises from Chapter 5 to calm your nervous system. When you're flooded with disappointment or anger, your thinking brain goes offline. You need to get regulated before you can learn anything useful from the experience.

Next, apply the reframing strategies we covered earlier. Instead of "I'm terrible at this," try "I'm learning what doesn't work." Instead of "I'll never succeed," try "I haven't succeeded yet."

The Resilience Bank Account

Every time you bounce back from a setback, you're making a deposit into your resilience bank account. These deposits compound over time, strengthening you for future challenges. The small failures you recover from today prepare you for bigger challenges tomorrow.

Elizabeth failed her driving test twice before passing on the third try. Each failure taught her something specific—the first time she learned to check her mirrors more consistently, the second time she practiced parallel parking until it was automatic. By the time she took the test a third time, she felt confident because she had systematically addressed her weak spots. More importantly, she learned that failure isn't permanent, and that persistence pays off.

Setting Up Your Next Chapter

As we prepare to explore living your truth and building your identity in the final chapter, remember that your relationship with failure will shape your entire future. People who fear failure stay small and safe. People who learn from failure grow bold and confident.

The emotional regulation skills you've developed throughout this book—recognizing triggers, managing intense emotions, communicating effectively, and bouncing back from setbacks—are all preparing you for something bigger. They're preparing you to live authentically and pursue the life you actually want, not just the safe one.

Your failures aren't roadblocks. They're stepping stones leading you toward the person you're becoming.

Befriend Yourself Through Daily Rituals

Throughout this book, we've tackled the big emotional challenges—rejection, anxiety, anger, and failure. But there's one relationship that affects every other area of your life: the one you have with yourself. After weathering the storms we discussed in the previous chapter, it's time to learn how to be your own best ally through the power of daily self-kindness rituals.

You probably wouldn't talk to your best friend the way you talk to yourself in your head. When your friend makes a mistake, you're understanding and supportive. When you mess up, you might be harsh and critical. Self-kindness isn't about lowering your standards—it's about motivating yourself with encouragement instead of criticism, which actually works better for building confidence and resilience.

Building self-kindness requires practice because most of us learned to be our own worst critics. But just like any skill, the more you practice treating yourself with compassion, the more natural it becomes. Self-kindness routines help you develop this muscle through small, daily actions.

The Science Behind Self-Compassion

Research shows that people who practice self-kindness actually perform better under pressure and recover faster from setbacks. When you rebuke yourself, your brain activates the same stress response we learned about in Chapter 1. This floods your system with stress hormones that make it harder to think clearly and learn from mistakes.

Self-kindness activates your brain's care system. This creates the psychological safety you need to take risks, learn new things, and bounce back when things don't go as planned.

Building Your Self-Kindness Toolkit

Here are practical ways to befriend yourself through daily rituals:

- The Friend Test: Before saying something harsh to yourself, ask, "Would I say this to my best friend?" If not, rephrase it with the same kindness you'd show them.
- Daily Kindness Rituals: Leave yourself encouraging notes, give yourself a literal pat on the back after hard days, or create a "wins" list to review when you're feeling down.
- Affirmation Upgrades: Instead of generic positive statements, use specific, believable affirmations like "I'm learning to handle stress better" or "I'm brave enough to try new things."

Sarah used to call herself "stupid" every time she made a mistake in math class. She realized she should never talk to her friend that way, so she started catching herself and rephrasing. Instead of "I'm so stupid," she'd think, "Math is challenging for me, but I'm working on it." She also started writing herself a daily note of encouragement and putting it in her backpack. On tough days, finding those notes reminded her that she was on her own team, not working against herself.

The Progress Over Perfection Mindset

Remember the growth mindset concepts we've explored throughout this book? Self-kindness is the fuel that keeps that mindset running. When you're kind to yourself, you're more willing to try new things because you know you won't beat yourself up if you fail.

This connects directly to everything we've learned about emotional regulation. The breathing techniques from Chapter 5, the communication skills from Chapter 7, and the resilience strategies from our recent discussions all work better when you approach them with self-compassion rather than self-criticism.

Creating Your Personal Kindness Routine

Start small with one daily self-kindness practice. Maybe it's taking three deep breaths and saying "I'm doing my best" when you feel overwhelmed. Or writing one thing you're proud of each day before bed. The key is consistency, not perfection.

Marcus started each morning by looking in the mirror and saying, "Good morning, you're going to handle today well." It felt weird at first, but after a few weeks, he noticed he felt more confident starting his day. When he had a rough day at school, he'd say his morning encouragement, and it helped him bounce back faster.

Preparing for Your Future

As we prepare to explore living your truth and building your identity in the final chapter, remember that self-kindness is the foundation for authentic living. You can't build a meaningful life on a foundation of self-criticism and harsh judgment.

The emotional regulation skills you've developed throughout this book work best when paired with self-compassion. When you treat yourself with kindness, you create the inner safety needed to take the risks required for authentic living.

Your Pocket Rescue for Dark Days

Life doesn't send you a warning text before delivering its hardest hits. One minute you're feeling fine, the next you're dealing with a friendship explosion, family crisis, or personal disappointment that leaves you feeling completely overwhelmed. After everything we've learned about handling rejection and loss, it's time to create your personal survival toolkit for those moments when emotions feel too big to handle alone.

Just like you'd keep a first aid kit for physical injuries, having a mental health emergency kit helps you handle emotional injuries when they happen. This isn't about preventing bad days (they're part of life) but having a plan for getting through them without making things worse.

Your emergency kit should be personalized to what actually helps you feel better, not what you think should help. Some people need movement; others need stillness. Some need to talk it out; others need quiet time. The key is knowing what works for you before you need it, because it's hard to think clearly when you're in crisis mode.

Building Your Emergency Kit

Think of this as your emotional first aid supplies, broken down into categories that address different support:

- Physical Items: Keep comfort objects like stress balls, essential oils, cozy blankets, or photos that make you smile easily accessible for tough moments.
- Digital Resources: Create playlists for different moods, save screenshots of supportive texts, bookmark funny videos, or keep a folder of your own accomplishments on your phone.
- People Resources: Have a list of specific people to contact for different needs—who to call when you need to vent, who to text when you need distraction, and which adults to contact in serious situations.

Marcus created his mental health emergency kit after a rough week when his parents divorced and he felt completely unprepared to handle his emotions. His kit included a playlist called "Songs That Get Me," a stress ball shaped like a basketball, screenshots of encouraging texts from his older brother, and the phone numbers for his school counselor and a crisis text line. He kept some items in his backpack and others saved on his phone. The next time he had a panic attack at school, he knew exactly what to do: he went to a quiet bathroom, squeezed his stress ball while listening to his playlist, and texted his brother. Having a plan helped him feel less helpless and get through the moment without it spiraling into something bigger.

Quick Access Strategies

Remember the breathing techniques we learned in Chapter 5? Include those in your emergency kit too. Practice the 4-7-8 breathing method enough times that you can access it automatically when stress hits. The same goes for the grounding techniques from Chapter 6 and the reframing strategies from Chapter 2.

Your kit should also include reminders of your own strength. Keep a note on your phone listing times you've overcome difficulties before. When you're in crisis mode, your brain forgets that you've handled hard things successfully. Having evidence of your own resilience can be incredibly powerful.

Making It Work in Real Life

The best emergency kit is useless if you can't access it when you need it most. Keep some items in multiple places—your room, backpack, car, or with trusted friends. Make sure your digital resources are saved offline too, in case you don't have internet access during a crisis.

Practice using your kit during smaller stressful moments so you'll remember it exists when bigger challenges hit. If you wait until you're in full crisis mode to try these strategies for the first time, they won't be as effective.

Recap of Key Points

Resilience isn't about being tough all the time—it's about developing skills to bounce back when life knocks you down. Remember that embarrassing moments are universal and temporary, failures are data that help you improve, self-kindness is more motivating than self-criticism, and having a mental health emergency kit prepares you for tough days. Building resilience is like building muscle—it takes practice, but every time you bounce back from a setback, you're getting stronger.

Action Steps

- Write your last embarrassing moment and practice the reframe technique: how would you view this situation if it happened to a friend?
- Think of a recent failure or setback and identify three pieces of useful information you can extract from the experience.
- Choose one self-kindness routine to try this week, whether it's writing yourself encouraging notes or practicing the friend test when negative self-talk starts.
- Start building your mental health emergency kit by identifying three physical items, three digital resources, and three people who could support you during tough times.

Now that you've learned how to bounce back from setbacks and build resilience, it's time to focus on the bigger picture: living authentically and building the confidence to show up as your real self in the world. Chapter 10 will help you define what "strong" means to you, embrace what makes you unique, and start writing your own success story on your own terms.

Chapter 10: Living Your Truth–Identity and Future

When Ordinary People Choose Brave

True strength isn't about being fearless or never crying—it's about showing up authentically even when it's uncomfortable. Courage happens in quiet moments: raising your hand when you're unsure of the answer, apologizing when you've hurt someone, or asking for help when you're drowning. These micro-moments of bravery build the confidence muscle you'll need for life's bigger challenges.

The Apology Courage: Admitting when you're wrong takes more strength than defending a lie. It shows emotional maturity and builds trust in relationships.

The Help-Seeking Courage: Asking for support—whether academic, emotional, or practical—demonstrates self-awareness and breaks down the myth that independence means doing everything alone.

The Authenticity Courage: Showing up as your real self, even when it might not be popular, builds genuine connections and self-respect.

Paige used to think courage meant never showing weakness. When she failed her driving test for the third time, she felt like a complete failure. Instead of making excuses or hiding from her friends, she posted about it honestly: "Round 3 of driving test = epic fail. Parallel parking is apparently not my superpower. Trying again next month!" The response surprised her—dozens of friends shared their own driving disasters and offered encouragement. Her vulnerability became a bridge to deeper friendships and showed her that real strength comes from being honest about struggles, not pretending they don't exist.

Remember the emotional regulation skills from Chapter 1? They become your foundation for brave choices. When you understand that all emotions are valid—including fear, disappointment, and uncertainty—you stop seeing them as roadblocks and start viewing them as information. Your anxiety before speaking up in class isn't weakness; it's your nervous system preparing you to do something important.

The resilience strategies from Chapter 9 work hand-in-hand with everyday courage. Each time you bounce back from a small setback, you're training your brain to trust that you can handle bigger challenges. When Felix got rejected from the school play, he felt crushed but used his emotional regulation techniques to process the disappointment instead of spiraling into self-doubt. He asked the drama teacher for feedback and discovered his audition song choice didn't showcase his actual vocal range. That "failure" led to better song selection for the next audition and eventually landing a lead role in the spring musical.

Brave doesn't mean reckless.

Smart courage involves calculated risks based on your values and goals. Before making any brave choice, ask yourself: "Does this align with who I want to become?" If standing up to a bully might escalate physical danger, that's not the time for direct confrontation—seek adult support instead. If speaking your opinion in a group discussion might face some disagreement but helps advance an important cause you care about, that's worth the discomfort.

Daily Bravery Practice

Start small with these courage-building exercises:

- Monday Moments: Choose one slightly uncomfortable thing each Monday—sit with someone new at lunch, contribute to class discussion, or try a different route to school.
- Feedback Friday: Ask for honest feedback from someone

you trust about an area you want to improve.

- Apology Accountability: When you mess up (because everyone does), practice quick, genuine apologies without excuses or explanations.

- Help-Seeking Hour: Dedicate time each week to asking for help with something you've been struggling with alone.

The communication skills from Chapter 7 become crucial here. Brave conversations require clear boundaries, honest expression, and respectful listening. When Paige tells her best friend that constant negative venting was draining her energy, she used "I" statements and offered specific solutions: "I care about you, but I feel overwhelmed when our conversations focus only on problems. Can we balance venting time with positive updates too?"

Your brave choices create ripple effects beyond yourself. When you model authentic courage—admitting mistakes, asking for help, standing up for others—you give permission for people around you to do the same. Schools, families, and friend groups become psychologically safer when someone breaks the perfectionism cycle and shows that it's okay to be human.

The inner critic that whispers "you're not good enough" throughout this journey becomes quieter as you accumulate evidence of your own capability. Each brave choice—no matter how small—deposits proof in your confidence account that you can handle whatever comes next.

Your "Extra" is Your Superpower

Your quirks, intense interests, and unique perspectives aren't flaws to fix—they're features that make you irreplaceable. Society often pressures teens to blend in, but the most fulfilled people are those who embrace what makes them different. Whether you're obsessed with medieval history, write fan fiction, or have strong opinions about social justice, your "extra" qualities are often your greatest strengths waiting to be unleashed.

The Niche Interest Power: Your deep knowledge about something specific can become a career path, creative outlet, or way to connect with like-minded people globally.

The Intensity Advantage: Being passionate and caring deeply gives you the fuel to create change, build meaningful relationships, and pursue goals with determination.

The Judgment Shield: Developing scripts and mindset shifts to handle criticism while staying true to yourself protects your authentic self from conformity pressure.

Adrian was embarrassed by his love of musical theater in a school where sports dominated social status. He kept his passion secret until his English teacher encouraged him to audition for the school play. Despite worrying about judgment, he decided to own his interest. When classmates made comments, he responded with confidence: "Yeah, I love theater. It's actually pretty challenging—try memorizing twenty pages of dialogue while hitting dance moves." His authenticity attracted other creative students, and he found his tribe. By senior year, he was directing student productions and had earned respect for his unique talents rather than hiding them.

Remember the emotional regulation foundation from Chapter 1? Those "too much" feelings you learned to validate become your creative fuel and passion engine. When Brooklyn felt overwhelming excitement about environmental science, her family often tells her to "calm down" about climate change. Using her emotion regulation skills, she recognized that her intensity wasn't a problem to solve—it was energy to channel. She started an environmental club at school, organized community cleanups, and eventually earned a scholarship for environmental studies. Her "too much" became exactly enough to make real change.

The social anxiety strategies from Chapter 6 help you show up authentically even when your interests seem different from everyone else's. Before sharing your unique perspectives, practice the grounding techniques and positive self-talk you've learned. Remember that anxiety often accompanies growth and courage.

Your authentic self attracts the right people.

When you hide your true interests and opinions, you attract relationships based on a fake version of yourself. That's exhausting to maintain and leaves you feeling lonely even when surrounded by people. When you embrace your "extra" qualities, you naturally filter for friends who appreciate the real you.

Authenticity Action Plan

Transform your perceived flaws into superpowers with these strategies:

- Interest Inventory: List your passions without judgment. Include the weird ones, the unpopular ones, and the ones that feel "too nerdy" or "too intense."
- Strength Translation: For each interest, identify transferable skills. Love video games? You're developing problem-solving abilities and hand-eye coordination. Obsessed with true crime podcasts? You're practicing critical thinking and attention to detail.
- Community Connection: Find your people online and offline. Every interest has a community—from Reddit threads to local clubs to Instagram accounts dedicated to your passion.
- Confidence Scripts: Prepare responses for judgment. Practice saying things like: "It's not for everyone, but I really enjoy it" or "I know it seems unusual, but it makes me happy."

The communication skills from Chapter 7 become essential when sharing your authentic self with others. You don't need everyone to understand your interests, but you can express them clearly and confidently. When Brooklyn talked about her love for competitive knitting, she explains it with enthusiasm rather than defensiveness: "I know it sounds weird, but there's actually a whole competitive scene. It's like speed chess but with yarn, and the patterns are incredibly complex."

Your "extra" often becomes your edge in college applications, job interviews, and future relationships. Admissions officers and employers aren't looking for cookie-cutter candidates—they want people who bring unique perspectives and genuine passion to their communities.

The resilience strategies from Chapter 9 support you when authenticity feels risky. Each time you show up as your real self and survive the potential judgment, you build evidence that being different isn't dangerous—it's your differentiator.

Your weirdness is your wisdom. Your intensity is your impact. Your unusual interests are your unique offerings to the world.

Stop apologizing for taking up space with your authentic self.

Confidence Unleashed in Minutes

Confidence isn't something you're born with—it's a skill you can build through specific techniques that shift your mental and physical state. These tools work because they hack your nervous system, sending signals to your brain that you're capable and strong. The key is having go-to strategies you can use in moments when you need an instant confidence boost.

Power Pose Preparation: Spending two minutes in a confident physical position (hands on hips, chest open, chin up) before challenging situations literally changes your hormone levels and increases feelings of power.

The Hype Playlist Strategy: Curating three to five songs that make you feel unstoppable and listening before presentations, social events, or difficult conversations primes your mindset for success.

Mirror Pep Talk Mastery: Developing personalized affirmations and encouragement phrases to say to yourself creates an internal cheerleader that counters self-doubt.

Abigail discovered the power of her pre-game routine before student government speeches. She would lock herself in the bathroom, do power poses while listening to her confidence playlist (starting with "Confident" by Demi Lovato), then look in the mirror and say, "You've got something important to say, and people need to hear it." This five-minute ritual transformed her from a nervous wreck into a composed speaker. She started using variations of this routine before job interviews, first dates, and college presentations, always customizing it to fit the situation while keeping the core elements that worked for her.

Remember the emotion regulation skills from Chapter 1? They become your foundation for confidence building. When you understand that nervousness and excitement create nearly identical physical sensations, you can reframe pre-performance jitters as anticipation rather than fear. Your racing heart isn't warning you of danger—it's preparing you for action.

The resilience strategies from Chapter 9 support confidence building by helping you bounce back when techniques don't work perfectly. Some days, your power pose might feel silly or your playlist might not hit the same way. That's normal. The goal isn't perfection; it's having multiple tools in your confidence toolkit.

Quick Confidence Boosters

These techniques take five minutes or less and can be done almost anywhere:

- The Victory List: Before challenging situations, quickly list three recent accomplishments—big or small. Reminded yourself: "I aced that chemistry quiz, helped my friend through a tough time, and learned to parallel park."
- Future Self Visualization: Spend two minutes imagining yourself succeeding in the upcoming situation. Picture specific details: your confident posture, clear voice, and positive outcomes.
- Breathing Power: Use the four-seven-eight breathing technique (inhale for four counts, hold for seven, exhale for eight) to activate your parasympathetic nervous system and reduce anxiety.
- Confidence Clothing: Choose one item that makes you feel powerful—whether it's lucky socks, a favorite bracelet, or a shirt that fits perfectly. Physical comfort translates to emotional confidence.

The social anxiety strategies from Chapter 6 complement these confidence techniques perfectly. When Hudson had to give a presentation about his summer job experience, he combined power posing with the grounding techniques he learned for managing social anxiety. He stood in the hallway doing his confident stance while mentally naming five things he could see, four things he could hear, and three things he could touch. This dual approach calmed his nerves while boosting his sense of capability.

Your body language affects your mindset more than you realize. Research shows that confident postures increase testosterone and decrease cortisol within minutes. When you stand tall, make eye contact, and take up appropriate space, you're not just appearing confident—you're becoming confident.

Emergency Confidence Protocol

For moments when anxiety threatens to derail your confidence:

- Reset Breathing: Take three deep breaths, making your exhale longer than your inhale.
- Positive Self-Talk: Replace "I can't do this" with "I'm learning to do this" or "I've handled tough things before."
- Micro-Movements: Subtly adjust your posture—roll shoulders back, lift chin slightly, uncross arms.

The communication skills from Chapter 7 work hand-in-hand with confidence building. Clear, direct communication both requires and creates confidence. When you speak up for yourself or express your needs clearly, you're practicing confidence in action.

Building confidence is like training a muscle—it gets stronger with consistent practice, but you might feel sore at first. Each time you use these techniques and survive the discomfort of being visible, you're training your brain to trust that you can handle whatever comes next.

Your confidence grows through evidence, not dreaming.

Crafting Your Personal Victory Narrative

Real glow-ups aren't just about physical changes; they're about becoming the person you're. This involves defining success on your own terms, tracking growth in areas that matter to you, and creating a vision for your future self that excites and motivates you. Your success story isn't written by grades, followers, or other people's approval—it's written by how well you know yourself and how courageously you pursue what matters to you.

Personal Success Metrics: Identifying what achievement looks like for you specifically—whether that's creative expression, helping others, academic excellence, or building strong relationships—rather than accepting society's narrow definitions.

Growth Documentation: Keeping track of emotional milestones, overcome fears, improved relationships, and developed skills creates a record of progress that's easy to forget in day-to-day life.

Future Self Visioning: Writing letters to your future self, creating vision boards, or journaling about your ideal life helps clarify goals and motivates present-day actions.

Caleb realized his definition of success had been completely shaped by his parents' expectations until he started his own "glow up" tracking. Instead of just monitoring grades, he began noting moments when he stood up for friends, creative projects he completed, and times he chose kindness over popularity. He wrote monthly letters to his future self, describing his current challenges and dreams. Looking back after a year, he could see patterns of growth he never would have noticed otherwise—like how he'd gone from avoiding conflict to becoming someone friends came to for advice. This documentation helped him recognize his own transformation and gave him confidence to decide based on his values rather than others' expectations.

Building on the resilience strategies from Chapter 9, your personal victory narrative becomes evidence that you can handle whatever comes next. Each documented growth moment—whether it's using the anger management techniques from Chapter 5 during a family argument or applying the social anxiety tools from Chapter 6 to join a new club—proves you're developing real emotional regulation skills.

Your story isn't about avoiding difficulties.

The most interesting personal narratives include chapters about struggles, failures, and comebacks. When Lila looked back through her growth journal, she noticed her proudest moments weren't when everything went perfectly—they were when she bounced back from rejection, learned from mistakes, or chose courage despite fear. Her "failures" became plot points in a larger story of resilience and self-discovery.

Victory Narrative Framework

Create your personal success story using these elements:

- Values Clarity: Define your core values based on the self-awareness you've developed throughout this book. What principles guide your decisions when no one is watching?
- Progress Tracking: Document monthly wins, lessons learned, and moments when you used emotional regulation skills successfully. Include minor victories like

choosing not to react to drama or speaking up in class.

- Challenge Reframing: Write about setbacks as character development rather than plot holes. How did that friendship conflict teach you about boundaries? What did academic struggles reveal about your learning style?
- Future Visioning: Describe your ideal self in specific, actionable terms. Instead of "be more confident," write "speak up in meetings, set clear boundaries, and pursue opportunities that align with my values."

The communication skills from Chapter 7 help you articulate your growth story to yourself and others. When you can clearly explain how you've changed and what you've learned, you reinforce those positive changes and inspire others to pursue their own growth.

Remember the emotion basics from Chapter 1? Your "too much" feelings become the fuel for your transformation story. Maya's intense sensitivity, which once felt like a burden, became her superpower when she learned to channel it into writing poetry that helped other students feel less alone. Her emotional depth wasn't something to fix—it was something to harness.

Creating Your Success Timeline

Map your growth journey using these categories:

- Emotional Regulation Wins: Times you managed difficult emotions effectively
- Relationship Improvements: Stronger boundaries, better communication, deeper connections

- Courage Moments: Instances when you chose bravery over comfort
- Authenticity Achievements: Situations where you showed up as your real self
- Resilience Examples: How you bounced back from disappointments or failures

Your victory narrative isn't about comparing yourself to others; it's about recognizing your own evolution. The shy person who started reading this book might now be the one encouraging friends to try new things. The angry teen might now be the one helping others cool down conflicts.

Document your growth not to brag, but to remember your capability when future challenges make you doubt yourself.

Your story is still being written, and you hold the pen.

Conclusion

You picked up this book because something inside you knew you needed more than just "calm down" or "think positive." You needed real tools, honest conversations, and practical strategies that actually work in the messy reality of teenage life. Throughout these pages, we've built something powerful together: a comprehensive toolkit designed specifically for your unique challenges and strengths.

This isn't just another self-help book that promises to "fix" you because you were never broken to begin with.

Instead, we've created a roadmap for understanding your emotional world, honoring your sensitivity as the superpower it is, and developing the confidence to navigate everything from friendship drama to family conflicts to your own inner critic. Every technique, script, and strategy in this book has been crafted with one goal in mind: helping you become the expert on your own emotional life.

You now have the vocabulary to name what you're feeling, the tools to manage overwhelming moments, and the confidence to communicate your needs clearly and kindly. Most importantly, you have permission to be authentically, unapologetically yourself.

What We've Learned Together

Looking back through our journey, several key themes have emerged that change everything about how you experience your emotional life:

Emotions are information, not emergencies. Your feelings are trying to tell you something important about your needs, boundaries, or values. When you stop seeing emotions as problems to solve and start seeing them as data to understand, everything changes. That anxiety before a presentation? It's telling you this matters to you. That anger when someone interrupts you? It's protecting your need to be heard.

Sensitivity is a superpower when managed well. Your ability to feel deeply, notice subtleties, and empathize with others isn't a weakness—it's a strength that the world desperately needs. The key is learning to channel this sensitivity rather than being overwhelmed by it. Remember Sarah from Chapter 2, who learned to see her emotional awareness as her secret weapon for understanding people and situations?

You can learn to respond instead of react. There's always a pause between what happens to you and how you choose to respond. With practice, you can learn to find that pause and use it to make choices that align with your values rather than your impulses. This single skill transforms everything from arguments with friends to dealing with social media drama.

Your triggers are valid and manageable. Everyone has emotional triggers based on their unique experiences and sensitivities. Identifying your specific triggers isn't about avoiding them forever—it's about preparing for them and developing healthy coping strategies. When you know loud noises overwhelm you or that certain topics make you anxious, you can plan and take care of yourself.

Boundaries protect relationships. Setting limits isn't mean—it's how you maintain your energy and authenticity so you can show up fully for the people and activities that matter most to you. Healthy boundaries actually strengthen your relationships because people know where they stand with you.

Growth happens in spirals, not straight lines. You'll have good days and hard days, breakthroughs and setbacks. This isn't failure—it's the natural rhythm of human growth. Every spiral up brings you to a higher level of understanding and resilience.

Your Most Important Tools

As you move forward, keep these essential takeaways close to your heart:

- Name it to tame it - emotional vocabulary is power. The more specific you can be about what you're feeling, the more effectively you can address those feelings. "I feel overwhelmed by my math test tomorrow" gives you much more to work with than "I feel bad." Use the Mood Wheel, practice emotional check-ins, and build your feeling vocabulary like you're learning a new language—because you are.

- Your feelings are valid even when others don't understand. Just because someone else wouldn't react the same way doesn't mean your reaction is wrong. Your emotional responses are shaped by your unique brain chemistry, past experiences, and current circumstances. You don't need anyone else's permission to feel what you feel.
- Small daily practices create big changes. You don't need to overhaul your entire life overnight. Checking in with your emotions once a day, practicing one grounding technique, or using one communication script can create ripple effects that transform how you experience and navigate your world.
- Asking for help is brave, not weak. Recognizing when you need support and actually reaching out for it takes tremendous courage. Whether it's asking a friend to listen, requesting accommodations from a teacher, or seeking professional help, asking for support is a sign of self-awareness and strength.
- You get to define what success looks like for you. Success isn't just about grades, likes, or other people's approval. Maybe success means speaking up in class once this week, setting a boundary with a friend, or simply getting through a hard day without being mean to yourself. Your definition of success should align with your values, not society's expectations.

Your Next Steps Start Now

Don't let this book become just another thing you read and forget about. Your growth starts with action, even small ones.

Choose one technique in this book to practice this week. Don't implement everything at once. Pick one strategy that resonated with you—maybe it's the 5-4-3-2-1 grounding technique, the "pause before responding" practice, or daily emotional check-ins with the Mood Wheel. Practice it consistently for one week and notice how it affects your daily experience.

Create your mental health emergency kit today. Gather your comfort items, write your go-to coping strategies, and save important phone numbers in your phone. Include things like your favorite calming playlist, a soft blanket, stress ball, or fidget toy. Having these tools ready before you need them makes all the difference during overwhelming moments.

Share one tool with a friend who might need it. You probably know someone else who struggles with similar challenges. Share one technique that's been helpful for you—maybe teach them box breathing, send them the "assertive communication" scripts, or simply let them know they're not alone in feeling overwhelmed sometimes.

Practice one new boundary this month. Start small, but start somewhere. Maybe it's saying, "I need some time to think about it" instead of immediately saying yes to plans, asking for space when you're feeling overwhelmed, or letting family know you need an hour of quiet time after school to decompress.

Celebrate one thing that makes you "extra." Write down one quality about yourself that others might see as "too much" but that you're learning to appreciate. Maybe you feel things deeply, notice details others miss, ask thoughtful questions, or care intensely about causes that matter to you.

Own it, celebrate it, and remember that the world needs your particular brand of "extra."

The Truth About You

Your emotional intensity isn't a flaw to fix—it's a feature to celebrate and channel. In a world that often tells teenagers to tone it down, fit in, and stop being so dramatic, your willingness to feel fully and authentically is actually revolutionary. Your sensitivity allows you to notice things others miss, your empathy helps you connect deeply with people, and your passion drives you to care about things that matter.

You have everything you need inside you already; these tools just help you access your own wisdom and strength. Every time you pause before reacting, every time you name what you're feeling, every time you set a boundary or ask for help, you're practicing skills that will serve you for the rest of your life.

You're not just surviving your teenage years—you're building the foundation for a life lived authentically and courageously.

The world needs your authentic voice and sensitive heart. Don't let anyone convince you to dim your light or shrink yourself to make others comfortable. Instead, use these tools to shine brighter, love deeper, and show up more fully as exactly who you are. Your future self is already proud of you for picking up this book and doing the brave work of understanding yourself better.

Remember: you are not too much. You are not too sensitive. You are not broken or dramatic or any of the other labels that might have been placed on you. You are a human being with a rich inner world, valid feelings, and valuable perspectives.

You deserve to take up space, to be heard, and to be loved exactly as you are.

Keep growing, keep feeling, and keep being beautiful, authentically you.

Resources for Teens

If you're struggling, overwhelmed, or dealing with emotions that feel too heavy to manage alone, you are not expected to handle everything by yourself. Support is real, available, and designed for teens just like you. Reaching out is a sign of strength, not weakness.

When to Reach Out for Professional Support

It may be time to talk to a counselor, therapist, doctor, or another trusted adult if you notice any of the:

- Emotions that feel too big or too constant

- Stress, sadness, or anger that lasts over two weeks

- Feeling disconnected, hopeless, or emotionally numb

- Panic attacks or anxiety that interrupt daily life

- Trouble functioning at school, at home, or with friends

- Using substances to cope with emotions

- Dramatic changes in sleep, appetite, or energy

- Thoughts about hurting yourself or feeling like you don't matter

24/7 Crisis Support (United States)

- 988 Suicide & Crisis Lifeline

- Crisis Text Line: Text HOME to 741741

- The Trevor Project: 1-866-488-7386 or text START to 678678

- SAMHSA National Helpline: 1-800-662-HELP (4357)

If You Live Outside the United States

Visit https://www.opencounseling.com/suicide-hotlines to find international hotlines. If you feel unsafe, call your local emergency number immediately.

For Deeper Practice and Hands-On Tools

The Teen Emotional Wellness Workbook is the companion to this book and provides worksheets, reflection prompts, tracking tools, and emotional regulation exercises to help you deepen the skills you learned.

For continued growth in confidence, identity, and self-worth, the Teen Self-Esteem & Emotional Strength Guide offers additional strategies that build on the work you've done here.

Please Leave a Review

Thank you for spending your time and energy with this book. If these tools, stories, or strategies helped you in any way—even a small one—I would be incredibly grateful if you took a moment to leave a review.

Your review doesn't have to be long or complicated.A sentence or two about what you found helpful is more than enough.

Why it matters:

- Reviews help other teens (and parents) know this book is worth reading.
- They help the book reach the people who need it most.
- And they support authors who create resources like this one.

If you're willing, please take a moment to share your thoughts on Amazon or wherever you purchased the book. Your voice genuinely makes a difference.

Thank you for being here, for showing up for yourself, and for being part of this journey.I'm cheering for you always.

Warmly,

Agnes Blake

www.ingramcontent.com/pod-product-compliance
Ingram Content Group UK Ltd.
Pitfield, Milton Keynes, MK11 3LW, UK
UKHW041638190726
13854UKWH00006B/2571

9 798993 423241